AF240865

I Don't Want to Go to School Anymore

Thierry Delcourt

I Don't Want to Go to School Anymore

**Between refusal, phobia and dropping out:
Understanding to better help your child**

Max Milo

© Max Milo Editions

Collection Essais-Documents, Paris, 2023

www.maxmilo.com

ISBN : 978-2-31501-191-9

WHY DON'T YOU WANT TO GO TO SCHOOL?

I want more, I can't anymore: how far will this growing phenomenon go, as we will see? Why does a child no longer want to go to school or can't? The question is often difficult to grasp and to untangle. Fear, anxiety, phobia, intimidation, following violence, racketeering or harassment: these are the most frequent reasons, isolated or often associated with each other. However, we are currently witnessing an increase in more vague and debatable reasons for refusal: opposition, revolt, absenteeism which tends to lead to a complete drop-out, resignation for comfort and laziness, opportunism taking advantage of the lax application of rules in certain schools, contagion between friends who prefer to go elsewhere, as well as a break in the relationship, linked, for example, to an experience of failure or a family failure As in the world of work, there is also a more insidious form of dropping out, presenteeism (he is there without being there) through disinterest, laziness, without or under the effect of illicit substances.

The statistics published by the DEPP (Direction de l'évaluation, de la prospective et de la performance) give us very little data from the National Education Department on the subject of absenteeism and dropping out. There is no specific analysis or precise figures on school blocking and refusal. However, by cross-checking these data with those of the CNED, Centre national d'enseignement à distance, we can get a small idea of this phenomenon that interests us. In the year 2021, the CNED treated two hundred and fifty thousand files which also correspond to other reasons, in particular medical, but the clear increase of its activity corresponds especially to the deschooling on the grounds of school phobia which makes it possible to profit from its services free of charge. To this can be added the increase in the number of accommodation measures proposed by the National Education in the framework of the Apadhe, pedagogical support at home, in hospital or at school, replacing the Sapad, pedagogical assistance service at home. The cooperation between teachers, school management and national education doctors allows for an adaptation that adjusts to the needs of the student in difficulty. In addition, some schools have made inventive proposals to adapt to the student's difficulties as closely as possible. Outside of the school setting, there has also been a significant increase in IEF (instruction in the family), which is why the prefects and the National Education Department have increased their controls. Let's add to this a nebula of new, unprecedented and increasingly frequent situations. In this case, the expectation of school support and care obliges the child to tinker at home and often to miss or limit schooling because the child is in pain, disrupts the class and as a result is stigmatized and expelled from a system that would like to be inclusive without being able to be so.

All the education and health care professionals I interviewed also note the increase in school dropouts, and this at an increasingly early age in secondary school. The government is tackling this problem with varying degrees of success, proposing a number of light, alternative and professional measures, but without succeeding in stemming the tide of heavy absenteeism and dropout.

Qualitative analysis is more enlightening than quantitative trends, even if it is valuable to be able to put numbers on it. This would merit a national evaluation, which would not be an easy task, given the diversity of situations and alleged reasons for dropping out of school. If we attempt to extrapolate the above-mentioned data on phobias and anxious refusals of school, dropouts and prolonged absenteeism from the various organizations, we can estimate the extent of the disaster at around 800,000 pupils who are dropping out of school for all reasons. As for the evolution, my interviews with school doctors, state truancy and dropout monitors, teachers, doctors, psychiatrists, child psychiatrists and psychologists, confirm the resurgence of school dropouts, often for debatable, sometimes inadmissible reasons. The answers to the questionnaire I sent them confirm that the cases they have to deal with have increased by about 10% during the year 2021-2022. This means that out of the twelve million French students, nearly 8% would be affected by de-schooling. However, this percentage, which is based on extrapolations, does not reflect objective data that would be necessary, if only to implement effective measures to curb this phenomenon.

What about the current growing problem of refusal, blocking, inability to face school, teachers, students or some of them? The phenomenon is not new but it is becoming very worrying because of its galloping expansion confirmed by health and education professionals?

After all, why force oneself to go to school when one can stay *at* home, go out and play with friends, be protected from the trials of life? Especially since, as the school public (children, parents and many teachers) can testify, the standardized functioning of the school, the rigidity in the application of the programs, the obsession with evaluating everything, the race for performance paradoxically associated in practice with a relaxation of school requirements and the automatic passage from class to class regardless of the results, bear responsibility for the amplification of the phenomenon of dropping out. Let's add to this the evolution of society, of the relationship to authority, of the family structure and its educational framework, of the place of the media and of the growing addiction to screens and social networks. Let's add to this the choice of some parents who want a different school education for their child who is different (or whom they think is different). According to the school's opinion or their own, he/she struggles and fails to adapt. This is a reality linked to the government's desire to include children in school, regardless of their difficulties. However, this is done without a real adaptation of the school environment and the educational programs. Another impasse that can lead to school refusal is the very, even overly protective emotional and educational posture of parents who take the initiative to withdraw their child from school and provide family instruction (IEF) according to their method, which they consider better, which is debatable, or more often by drawing inspiration from alternative pedagogies. A more worrying phenomenon that requires monitoring by government services is the decision to remove a child from school, which may be based on a community or religious ideology, in order to keep the child away from school, which is considered to be deviant and amoral, and to educate him or her according to the principles and precepts of their community.

The interplay of all of these factors clearly has a formidable effect on the proper functioning of school learning and the results that are expected. It is in this spirit that the government has tightened the rules for family instruction, home schooling and the approval of non-contractual schools. The law reinforcing the principles of the Republic, promulgated in August 2021, imposes a legal framework that limits authorizations (see appendix, at the end of the book) and controls, upstream and downstream of the authorization, the pedagogical quality and effectiveness of the teaching.

The fact remains that anxiety, a major problem in school dropout, invites itself without warning. It constitutes a trauma that forces the child to flee in order to prevent it from happening again. To flee where it has manifested itself, in this case to the school which, even if it is not the only source of the anguish, becomes the alleged reason, the cause by a psychic process of phobic displacement. This is followed by an avoidance behaviour that focuses on the school. We understand the difficulty in identifying and resolving this knot around the initial event of the anxiety. How can one find one's way through and help a child who is unable or unwilling to go through the school gate, which he sees as a prison or a threatening place, or worse, a place of torture?

Here is a small selection of what I hear during consultations for school refusal: *School sucks, you don't learn anything; Anyway, I won't make it; We're not rich, school is not for us; Teachers, those bastards, they humiliate us, we don't give a fuck about them; At school, we all suck, we don't want to learn, the teachers keep saying it, that's how it is; Every time I arrive in front of the school, my stomach hurts and I want to vomit; I can't help it, I can't get through the gate, I don't understand; There are boys who bother me, I'm afraid; School is too hard; I don't want to leave my mom, I have to stay close to her; I feel too bad in class, it's as if I'm suffocating; The teachers do surprise tests, it stresses me out, I'm afraid I won't make it; The older kids hit us and the teacher doesn't say anything; I don't like to work; I don't know who's going to come and pick me up, once they even forgot about me.*

Through these children's comments, we hear that these blocks and refusals cover very diverse situations. Societal, educational, psychosocial and psychological dimensions are involved. This is difficult to untangle for parents, schools and doctors, a little less so for child psychiatrists and psychotherapists who take the time to listen to children and their parents, if possible without *preconceived ideas* and with respect.

The Covid pandemic, the fear of contagion, the social distancing, the confinement have upset the social references, the rhythms, the relationships between children, between teenagers, with their parents and in their socio-school life. Distance learning was improvised and it worked as well as it could, especially since, at the same time, teleworking was imposed on parents. This situation was hard on most people, but it also allowed them to experience new situations of relaxation, a calming of the pace of life, a certain comfort that they had become accustomed to, and also to experience warm moments and attractive devices that changed their relationship to work and to learning at school, and that also opened up other forms of relationship within the family and with teachers. In addition to this imposed change, digital technology has become commonplace, both alone and on the network, and has expanded considerably as a work tool, sometimes in a jarring combination of fun, work and administrative dematerialization. As far as the children are concerned, the teachers have noted that this has led to a pedagogical discontinuity with a loss of social equity linked to various fractures. First of all, parents are not teachers, even less so if they have not been taught, and are sometimes even illiterate. Another obstacle is the digital divide due to the lack or failure of the network, especially in the countryside, or due to the malfunctioning of the domestic connection system. Even more unfair, linked to the loss of equity caused by the disparity in living conditions, housing and educational support, no one was ready for distance learning and this has served many children poorly.

Thus, children, parents and teachers have experienced at various levels a demobilization that has gone as far as discouragement and dropping out of school, from which it has sometimes been very difficult to recover. Some media speak of a *great resignation,* resulting from the pandemic, which has led many people, including teenagers, to question a lifestyle centered on work, or even to refuse it. Without going so far as to subscribe to such a hasty conclusion, we note that it corresponds in part to reality, including for teachers who are put to the test in this forced adaptation, and who are nevertheless supposed to give the desire to learn. They have to push their recalcitrant pupils all the more to make an effort to acquire a common base of standardized knowledge. Because of their abstraction and their methodological complexity, this knowledge is no longer really in phase with the ways of thinking and the concerns of children and adolescents. Should they be adapted and should pedagogy be adapted? Can the current resignation lead to a reorganization of school learning inspired by the societal reorganization linked to the pandemic?

It is only partly true that "it is Covid's fault" because these blockages and refusals to attend school were already a strong trend before this exceptional pandemic situation. It would be better to speak of the aggravation of a more complex phenomenon of questioning, failure, and opposition in the obligation of children to ensure their presence and learning at school. Obviously, the obligations from which children in the last century rarely derogated no longer have the same importance. There is a phenomenon of escape that poses a real problem, both societal, educational and psychosocial. Still, many parents ask for emergency consultations, in disarray when faced with their child's inability to attend school, when they are criticized by their entourage and the school for not being able to ensure their child's schooling, judging them to be lacking in authority and responsibility. However, most of the time, they are overwhelmed and suffer from the situation, even if some of them are sometimes accomplices of the de-schooling for a more or less fallacious reason (ideological, religious, by hyperprotection) or initiators for a reason that they consider legitimate (failing school, deviance of harassing pupils or mistreating teachers)

Why don't you want to go to school? This is the question that is asked of the child. Generally, he doesn't know or he is unable to answer. He or she wonders what is going on and often does not understand. Parents, brothers and sisters, teachers, school administrators, doctors and psychologists all ask questions, sometimes empathetic, sometimes annoyed or reproachful. In other words, the child's discomfort increases with the pressure and insistence of a question that, when asked in this way, is not really judicious.

In order to explore the diversity of situations, to make them explicit and to propose the best response to the child, his parents and the school environment, I have chosen to start from the words of these children in difficulty who come to consult and try to describe what they are experiencing. They are asked two questions by parents and people who want to help them: *Why don't you want to go? What are we going to do?* While the child's tentative answer is important, it is not enough to understand what the problem really is or to find an easy solution to the blockage.

Like a number of shrinks, I take care to welcome and listen to the child and his parents with attention and without *a priori* judgment.

I ask for their active participation. The child's participation is essential to solve the problem, whatever it may be. In order to understand the real reason for the dropout and not to be mistaken in the attitude to have according to the situation, I make each case a particular case. That is why I develop so many situations, limiting myself to the most frequent ones. In order for the reader (parent, child, professional) concerned by this problem to find his or her way around, I leave out a few singular details so that he or she can refer to a situation that is more or less similar to the one he or she is familiar with. This book is a toolbox in which everyone will find, I hope, their own situation and personalized answers thanks to the key title of each chapter, in the form of a word spoken by the student who no longer passes through the school gate.

The first part, "It's not that I don't want to, it's that I can't", a classic that is still relevant today, deals with various forms of anxious school blocking. It focuses on describing and understanding the phenomenon of anxious refusal, the child's suffering and his inability to go to school. This remains the main problem for the child and his or her disoriented parents. They are often very alone to face this painful situation.

The second part, *"It's okay, I quit, I want more"*, is very current and growing, and focuses on the refusal to submit to school. It deals with situations of exhaustion and refusal to perform. I also talk about children who suffer from a masked situation of social and psycho-affective suffering, as well as cases of devaluation, failure and dropping out. I wonder about the rebels who oppose and refuse to submit to the school constraint like others. These new problems of school refusal are very embarrassing for the parents, teachers and caregivers who are called upon, but without posing any real problem for the children concerned, at least in appearance.

The third part, "Should we trust the solutions found by the child?" analyzes what children sometimes propose when they are out of school or in the process of being out of school. It is worth looking into, while remaining vigilant about the appearance of a good solution that can quickly turn out to be a false good solution, or even a very bad one. These ideas can be surprising, opportunistic or idealistic. They may be pragmatic and able to deal with their inability, their giving up or their refusal to go to school. Some of these children are very good at using their intelligence to spare their efforts by staying on the bangs of the school system. Others want the school system to adapt to their difficulties and seek to use the possibilities of accommodation that interest them if their objective is not to break with learning.

Each chapter in the first two parts ends with a box entitled "Saying and Doing" which is intended for parents and professionals. It contains advice that has its limits but can be a complementary tool to help the child in the best possible way. These guidelines for speaking and acting are always linked to the clinical situation of the chapter, where they can find more or less the situation experienced with their child.

I - It's not that I don't want to, it's that I can't

That's it, my child can't, can't take it anymore, he suffers, we have to believe him because it's neither a whim nor a staging. Something imposes itself on him, suddenly or progressively, it overwhelms him, it acts in him as if he was traumatized. His body is crossed by painful sensations that he has never known before or that he has already known but had remained buried deep inside, and it reappears like a tsunami. It overwhelms him or it crushes him, he can't take it anymore and would be ready to do anything, even the worst, to escape from his anguish which takes various forms: sensation of falling into a black hole, unbearable thoracic constriction, lump in the throat, impossible swallowing, nausea, vomiting... The first anguish crisis is terrible, one doesn't get used to it. On the contrary, the psyche sets up a defensive device which is mainly translated by anxiety, a warning signal often named "stress", wrongly, which leads to the avoidance of all that could wake up the anguish which acts like a traumatism. However, the child does not know what triggered it and even less its cause, so everything becomes a source of anxiety. His behavior seems irrational, between phobic flight attitude, compulsive rituals, aggressiveness if we try to go against his defense against anxiety, DCA effective but which paralyzes him. He can even have a panic attack and put himself in danger if he has to go through the school gate. He risks being run over because he is capable of crossing the road suddenly. He goes so far as to hit the person who wants to let him in. He screams, not in anger but in pain, in fear. One cannot understand him until one has experienced the devastation of anguish. The pain is as terrible as it is unfounded in the eyes of others, even to the point of taking one's own life to make it stop. It is a serious matter that must be taken seriously. If reassurance is useful, it is not enough to soothe the crisis of anxiety, of panic, the ins and outs of which remain an enigma for the helpless parents, at the risk of acting awkwardly and aggravating the problem. Let's look at these problems, the issues at stake, the support and care that each of us can provide to these children in real suffering.

I have a stomach ache, I'm afraid to vomit

I receive in consultation very worried parents who accompany their only daughter aged 8 years, thin, pale face, on the verge of tears, visibly frightened by the situation. I start by reassuring her and ask the parents to explain the situation: they were called by the teacher who could not console their daughter in panic, who was crying and screaming in the classroom until she vomited. This happened suddenly without any warning. No one understood what was going on. The mother came home with her daughter clinging to her. As soon as she walked away, it was panic all over again. During the weekend, the mother took care of her daughter, comforted her, tried to understand her. No clue nor event, the child undergoing this major anguish without being able to say anything other than: *I am afraid... I am going to vomit, do not leave me.* On Monday morning, the departure is done without difficulty but, arrived at the school, she is again taken of panic. The mother and the teacher reassure her. When, exhausted, the teacher takes her by the hand, the cries redouble and she bites her arm. She has to face the facts, entering the school is beyond her strength and triggers an aggressive survival reaction. The mother met with the attending physician who prescribed a small herbal remedy and a sick leave for the child. In the following days, there is no question of the daughter or the mother leaving the house. Nightmares and permanent anxiety are added to this, especially since the father, annoyed, uses his big voice. The situation is blocked and the child can only repeat that she is afraid. The following days, taken of nauseas in front of food, she practically does not eat any more and repeats in loop: *I am afraid to vomit.* The nights were chaotic: waking up, calling her mother, enuresis episode which plunged the child into distress. Depressive signs come to complicate the manifestations of anguish. The doctor carries out a check-up, prescribes an anti-emetic and advises the parents to meet a psychiatrist. I meet her after two exhausting weeks for her and her parents.

We enter the heart of the matter in order to understand what is at stake in this anxiety. The parents, warm and open, are very worried about their daughter, who has been jovial but reserved until now. They see her wasting away, they imagine the worst, a trauma, an aggression. They think that something serious has escaped them. The anguish is shared and accentuated on both sides. Their daughter has lost 2 kg, no longer plays, no longer goes to the dance. She refuses to meet her girlfriend, withdraws to the living room couch, does not leave her mother's sight. Two problems arise: the imminent danger and the psychic resolution of the anxiety. The prescription of an anxiolytic is necessary to stop the escalation of the evil. I ask the parents and the daughter for their agreement and she nods her head and agrees. Once this is established, we explore not the reason for the anxiety, but its context. It is useless to ask the question for the umpteenth time why the anxiety and the refusal to go to school, the answer would be the same: *I am afraid, I am afraid to vomit.* The context is the present and the history of this little girl, the meaning of her discomfort and the way the parents react. In this situation, they feel guilty, especially the mother who unwinds her alleged faults:

I - It's not that I don't want to, it's that I can't

"We had her late and I thought I was going to lose her at birth...
I didn't want another child, I was too afraid. I was very protective
of her, maybe there was a break when I went back to work. In fact, I
shouldn't have.

His daughter listens attentively, I call out to her:

- What do you think of what your mother is telling us?

She frowns and clings to her:

- You see, she can't leave me.

She whispers in his ear:

- I'm sorry, Mom, I don't want to bother you, I'm not nice.

I invite the father to speak up too:

- I work a lot, so I don't get to play with her much. It's mostly her mom
who takes care of her...she's a mother hen."

I joke, smile and try to communicate with the child, a delicate
moment. She has to feel that I am close to her, to her parents and
that I don't want to hurt her in any way, including putting her back to
school, which is not the case. This first contact is essential if we do not
want the defensive construction to drag on and the child to get stuck in
her regression in search of maternal security in the face of a world that
has become threatening. It is necessary to shift and surprise her while
reassuring her, so that the external world loses its dimension of threat.
This detour must allow to soothe by deceiving the defenses (the fear of
vomiting, the fear of the school, the ritual of protection), and to reveal
the association of imaginary unconscious ideas which produced the
anguish, whether there was an aggression or not. I therefore start from
the principle that every detail is important because it is from a detail
that everything is a *priori* set on fire. Even if there is no aggression,
sexual trauma, humiliation, harassment, anxiety can be present, but
we never rule out the hypothesis of a serious event.

It is not possible or possible to tackle the problem head on. So I talk
to her about things, ask her what cartoons she watches, if she talks with
her friend. I am interested in her games, her dreams, her vacations, her
best present, and I gradually get to what might have been bothering her

at school. We know that there are so many stories between the children, that they share their fears. We know that they listen to their parents, and what is said, misunderstood, in a heated discussion can create a lot of insecurity. But it is also possible that she has seen something that has worried her, traumatized her in a cartoon or shocking images surreptitiously seen on television.

After a few sessions, it suddenly came out: *At school, they made us do exercises. You have to hide under the tables without making noise, and I wanted to cough. I was afraid that the terrorists would kill me... I saw them on TV, they kill children.* Certainly, she is not the only student who exhibits or reinforces anxiety as a result of these exercises, even if the teacher does not overdo the awkward dramatization. Nor is she the only one who exhibits anxious phobic school refusal as a result of these exercises that are probably necessary as part of the precautionary principle. In other words, achieving this revelation is only the first step in overcoming her anxiety.

The subsequent interviews with the parents, and then alone with her, made it possible to build a bridge by starting from her fragility linked to an immaturity that is not pathological at her age. Accentuated by a maternal protection that has so far prevented her from confronting the reality of the world, the shock is all the stronger, to the point of trauma. The aim of the bridge is to enable the child to acquire an active position in order to face the world and the others, who are known to be unkind and do not spare naïve, fragile and different people. The bridge offered by psychotherapy is not intended to harden the person and keep him or her unaffected by the afflictions of our world. The goal is to allow the expression of emotions and fantasies about the worst that could happen. This is the prerequisite for becoming an actress, i.e. able to defend herself and act so that there is no longer a gulf between the family cocoon and the outside world. It is her awareness and her active position that, in a way, will allow her to domesticate reality.

It remains to return to school, which supposes to manage to dissociate the school environment from the interior insecurity. The

I - It's not that I don't want to, it's that I can't

resumption was progressive in the presence of his mother, sometimes of his father. They participated in class moments. In addition to the mobilization of the girlfriends to welcome her, she made a cake for her teacher, who was very attentive to her comfort. The teacher proposed creative activities that allowed the class to regain its function as a play area and the little one to take part in their organization, to bring her decorative touch in agreement and in complicity with the teacher. All of this required time and commitment from everyone. The fear of vomiting and the nausea lasted for part of the school year and the absences, well tolerated by the school, allowed her to maintain a decompression chamber. The following school year, a signal anxiety occurred, testifying to the insecurity and trauma produced by the first anxiety, if it was the first one, because the origin could have escaped the insight of his attentive mother.

Everything was done to take care of this little girl, so the clinical evolution took place in the best way with a quality of accompaniment of the parents, the teacher, the attending physician and the psychologist. None of them judged the withdrawal from school and the care was centered, not on the return to school at all costs, but on the preliminary return to inner security and the construction of a creative capacity necessary to gain confidence. This is far from always being the case, many situations drag on and the installation of a lasting school phobia forces the child to be taken out of school, sometimes for years. In any case, it is important to know that the scar of indelible anxiety is always ready to be reawakened in unexpected situations, and before they can be mastered.

As for the danger, the word is not too strong, it can go much further than biting the teacher's arm and settling into anorexic behavior. If the parents insist that the child return to school, make him/her feel guilty, blame him/her for a behavior that is beyond him/her, then the anguish gets worse and he/she may take it out on him/herself. So many times, parents have consulted me, distraught, because their child had turned a knife on himself or had locked himself in his room and wanted to jump out the window. Anxiety can lead to such self-destructive acts until a final act. A school refusal charged with strong anxiety is not to be taken lightly. Just as we give a sick leave to an adult who is suffering, we must accept to do so for a child who, because of his anxiety, is not able to enter a class and even less to assimilate school knowledge.

Saying and doing: understanding and protecting your child

The younger a child is, the more impressionable, vulnerable and impressionable he or she is. It is important to be aware of this if preventive measures (terrorism, fire) are imposed on them or if they are given civic, sexual and other information, even if it is justified.

The precautionary principle requires protection techniques in the face of risks that the child does not always understand and that can terrorize him. It is therefore necessary to prepare them and to know how to give up temporarily for certain fragile or different children.

Since teachers are not psychologically trained, they are not in a position, except as individuals, to prevent the traumatic shock effect of the prevention guidelines they are required to impose on children. Parents must have a say in this.

It is up to the parents to take the time to answer the child's questions, and even to ask them, so as not to let a traumatic shock, a source of anguish, set in.

Children should not be exposed to violent content, whether it is conversations, media intrusion, video content or console games. It is up to parents to ensure this, to be mindful of the recommended minimum age logos and to explain to their child why they are respecting this limit, even if their buddy is not subject to this same rule, due to laxity on the part of the parents. It is their role of protection and educational authority.

When I'm in class, I'm suffocating, I have to get out

Another frequent and painful case, a 14 year old teenager consulted us because he was experiencing a total mental block. For three months, he had not been going to school. A good student, studious, he would like to go but he can't help it, as soon as he gets ready, an anxiety attack with nausea, dizziness and panic occurs. This leads him to bang his head against the walls until he hurts himself. He blames himself, punishes himself, is sad and experiences it as an insurmountable impasse. He repeats to anyone who will listen that he does not understand what is happening to him. He apologizes to his parents. Suicidal thoughts appeared, which he confided to his mother and his doctor, who saw him at the first attack of anxiety and carried out a biological check-up, which turned out to be normal. Disarmed, he tried to play it down, to reassure the teenager and the parents. But faced with the insistence of the anxiety, which took the form of school phobia, he prescribed a light anxiolytic treatment. He advised him to meet a psychologist, who tried a cognitive type of psychotherapy acting on the automatism of anxious anticipation and negative thoughts. After two months without any convincing results, the doctor concluded that it was necessary to meet a child psychiatrist, from whom the adolescent and his parents had high expectations. This expectation is a burden for the practitioner but it is also the guarantee of a commitment from the young person, which will be confirmed during our meetings.

What kind of commitment is this? The human psyche is complex and, like an iceberg, the submerged, unconscious part, what we do not know about ourselves, is more important than what appears on the surface, directly accessible to consciousness. This is where the commitment lies, which obliges one to question what one does not know in order to discover what it is and the symptoms, the anguish that this produces. The process requires energy and time, which is not much appreciated in a society of immediate efficiency that prefers a surface treatment made of positive reinforcement, cognitive correction and drug prescription. In this teenager's case, this does not work, or it is not enough. The prescription of an effective anxiolytic is essential, and, in view of the depressive evolution, an antidepressant may prove useful at a later stage. But we begin, like wreck hunters, to locate the elements that will lead us to the origin of the incomprehensible appearance of a sensation of suffocation so intense that it obliged the teenager to leave the classroom urgently to go, staggering, to the infirmary, supported by a friend. It should be noted that he is a year ahead of his classmates, he is a very good student and, until then, was not really stressed, like others, by the prospect of the brevet des collèges. Of course, he works a lot, goes out little, rarely plays sports, preferring his room and books. He has two friends and is considered a nerd by the others, who avoid him. He prefers to avoid the usual distractions and conversations of older students, whom he considers a bit immature. Passionate about astronomy, he documents himself and would like to make a career out of it. It is all the more infuriating and desperate for him not to be able to enter the school. And yet it is not for lack of trying. Every morning for a month, he got up, dressed in spite of the anguish and the dizziness, and he asked his mother to drive him. Seeing him deteriorate day by day, she tried to reassure him, even suggesting that he organize his curriculum at home in agreement with the college. His friend, who was empathetic, brought him the lessons every day. There was no question of giving up, he continued to study in spite of everything.

In psychotherapy, a turning point came when we deciphered the fear of others' gaze, what they might think of him to make him so panicked.

"People look at me and judge me, it makes me feel bad.

- But what could they find out, you have a flaw... or you are at fault?

Big anguish, silence, then he speaks again about the fact of being judged as a nerd, of being isolated, against which I argue by specifying to him that, even if it is painful and hurtful, that does not prevent him from being used to it and that it does not justify his so brutal panic. He replies that he is being persecuted, that he is fed up, and then gets angry. I remain stoic and ask him to look again.

I - It's not that I don't want to, it's that I can't

- If I tell you, you'll judge me too... Yesterday I realized what was happening to me... it's a shame, I'm a rotten, disgusting."

He gets up and runs away. No news for a week, I decide to call his mother. She informs me that he does not leave his room anymore. She is very worried. I tell her to demand that he comes with her for a consultation. This moment of crisis, which is not without risk, can become a moment of denouement. This is what makes people say that they get worse by going to see a psychiatrist. The risk is not to open the Pandora's box but to stop there, to flee in order not to see what is inside. Intelligent, he will quickly understand the interest of not letting go of the case. I ask him to write down what he doesn't dare to tell me. The very next day, I receive an e-mail where he explains that he is very interested in physics but also in his teacher's physique. He feels more and more in love, which disturbs the listening of his course. But the worst was that while masturbating the face of his teacher appeared to him. He imagined her naked, fantasized about having sex with her, once, then twice... then every night when he got home from college. The strangest thing is that he didn't make the connection between this embarrassing situation that was troubling him and his judgment of himself projected onto the gaze of others. His persecutory mechanism was equal to his feeling of guilt, to the point of provoking anxiety attacks. The rest of the psychotherapy dealt with his feelings of guilt, the differences and similarities with other teenagers, his sexual desires and fantasies for someone he admired... and who was his mother's age. He was finally able to de-dramatize, i.e. to untie the trap he had set for himself by directing his desire towards this woman who, in addition to being beautiful in his eyes, was a professor of physics, a subject to which he was destined. The anxious manifestations practically disappeared. It was possible for him to return to college, but on the condition that he did not meet this woman. Accommodation was not a problem, as the college was willing to do anything to facilitate his return. Psychotherapy continued, leading him to make room for his desire to love a young woman by overcoming his Oedipal immaturity.

With this case, we measure the complexity of what is hidden behind an anxiety attack, a traumatic event, and therefore the process of avoidance that leads to a phobia without, as we say, a mother being able to find her young. It is the function of the phobia to displace the anguish on an element which, from near or far, refers to the source. One more step and it is a compulsive behavior of avoidance and rituals in order to stop the anguish from waking up. In his case, given the burden of guilt, a process of traumatic dissociation, which goes beyond simple denial, prevented this adolescent from making the connection between his sexual fascination with his teacher and the persecutory anxiety. So much so that I came to believe, prior to his revelation, that this was an entry into schizophrenia. Fortunately, it was just a neurotic anguish such as we frequently encountered in the 20th century, and which we tend to forget, wrongly, in a society which seems to be freer in its approach to desire and sexuality.

If, for him, the outcome was quite simple with the resumption of school five months after the first anxiety attack, for others one will come up against : *I don't understand, I don't know,* because the origin of the anxiety is buried, old, abstract, inaccessible. For example, an adult in failure took an infinite time to remember the remark of a teacher: *You, the pimply one, on the blackboard...* Laughed at by all the students, humiliated. And since then, his failure behaviour has only proved to him that he is ugly, lame and that he will never achieve anything. For another, an attack of infantile asthma had inscribed the anguish of unconscious death which woke up during a course of physical education and sport, after a roll where he had the breath cut. For another, it was the absence of a student who was said to be seriously ill that awakened a childhood anguish linked to an early hospitalization. In other words, it is sometimes necessary to look for a needle in a haystack, and above all not to be too quick to make the link of cause and effect between a current situation and the anxious refusal.

In the psychic construction of any person, even a harmonious one, there have been moments of anxious perplexity, of avoidance, of repression of an unwelcome fantasy, and also of events that have gone unnoticed but which have left their traumatic imprint. In other words, it should be possible to consider the anxiety attack and the anxious school refusal as symptoms that invite a review of the psychic construction. It is therefore a useful crisis, even if, of course, the person would have done without it. In fact, it is better if it manifests itself early in life, as it is easier to resolve during childhood than when an adult's defenses have become rigid, preventing access to more buried elements.

What is, in fact, a moment without going to school in view of the handicap generated by a reactionary formation, i.e. a "gas factory" of defense against one's unconscious thoughts which hinder cognitive and psycho-affective capacities throughout life? Certainly, it is distressing to see your child unable to go to school. He should be doing well, at his age, and school is compulsory! But let's never forget that if the necessary steps are taken through well conducted psychotherapy, he will benefit from this moment of painful anxiety. It is not a question of "what doesn't kill you makes you stronger", but of removing obstacles, identifying traumas and resolving them to open up to the world.

Saying and doing: preventing suicidal risk

Any indication or comment that suggests a risk of suicide should be taken seriously because the act of a teenager or pre-teenager is brutal and difficult to predict. We must therefore pay special attention to them, make ourselves available and take care of their discomfort and suffering.

If possible, and by choosing the right moment, one should talk about it without panicking. This is the best way to identify if it is a call to be listened to by arousing interest, or if the danger is imminent. This is also the best way to avoid using suicidal talk as a weapon to counteract educational needs.

If it is a call, it is crucial to help the young person express himself, without judging his attitude or what he is saying, without interrupting him to reassure himself because it is too difficult to hear, without interrupting him to reassure him even before he has understood.

If the danger is quite imminent, especially if the suicidal ideas are associated with attacks on the body, scarification, mutilation, this is a matter for the attending physician or child psychiatric emergency room.

Forcing a young person to return to school without having fully understood the reason for his blockage and begun to solve his problem increases the risk of suicidal acts. But letting him lock himself in his room and gradually become de-socialized carries the same risk in the more or less long term.

I can't tell you

Tom, 10 years old, in fifth grade, cannot and will not enter his school. As soon as he approached, he went into a spectacular fit, screaming and gesticulating. The father got angry and pulled him away by force. The child, out of his mind, hit him, screamed until the parents, exasperated, gave up. The scene was repeated several days in a row, getting louder and louder until they swooned. Faced with this total blockage, the parents, who were very busy at work, entrusted him to the grandmother. Tom slept a lot, crying every time he woke up, consoled by his grandmother. When he came home, the father deprived him of all his toys and made demeaning remarks, going so far as to tell him that he was not worthy of being his son, that he was a baby... which, of course, only made the situation worse. The mother, on the other hand, tried to talk to her son without success. When she insisted he let out an *I can't tell you*. It is in this deleterious context that I am brought to receive the child and his parents after an attempt of care at a psychologist which ended in a rupture because the father did not support to be questioned. The mother came alone with her son, sorry about this blockage and her husband's negative attitude.

I - It's not that I don't want to, it's that I can't

Three elements alert me: the school blocking with panic, the aggressiveness without words and the violence of the father towards his son in difficulty. During the first appointment, the mother explains the difficult family and professional context and the strong tension between the parents, stating:

"I can't talk in front of Tom.

To which I reply:

- So don't be surprised if he can't talk to you.

The mother insists on Tom's disorder.

- He became aggressive, he was usually so nice, and took on manias. He has developed a compulsion to wash his hands twenty times a day.

- If he is prevented from doing so, he will throw a fit.

The child is tense, agitated and sad. He says nothing, observes his mother and suddenly, crying, explodes:

- You don't know anything about me, you don't understand anything, I want to get out of here.

So I say:

- Your mother will go to the waiting room because you need to talk, but not in any way. Rest assured, I respect secrets."

He refuses and so we make an appointment, which he accepts, just after the winter vacations begin. I insist that the mother take the time to talk with her son and that we stop the deprivations and punishments that only aggravate the problem. A few days later, I receive a call from the father who vehemently demands to know why I did not diagnose and treat his son. We leave it at that.

Despite this, Tom comes to his appointment as soon as the school year starts, which he is unable to do. I ask him if he has managed to talk to his parents. He answers:

"Uh, yeah, they told me it wasn't right between them, that Dad was mad at Mom for having an affair. She said it was over. I heard them arguing, he was calling her a whore. They have their own problems and they don't care about me, so there's no point, I can't talk to them.

He explains that since the vacations he has become less anxious and has reduced his washing rituals, even though he still needs them.

- You'll have to tell me why you need it!

- But you won't tell anyone, so I can trust you?"

Respecting the secret is crucial because he is close to a painful revelation. He tells me that during recess, the bad guys in his class cornered him in the bathroom and forced him to undress, making fun of him. They left, telling him: *If you tell, we'll kill you.* Tom was left with this humiliation and fear in his stomach because he could not talk about it for fear of reprisals and the abuse would be repeated. His escape from school could have protected him, but the unavailability and tension of his parents did not allow him to create the conditions to talk about it, i.e. loving attention, the guarantee of silence and the protection to feel safe.

Tom is relieved to have spoken to me in secret but it is not possible to pass these serious aggressions under silence, neither with regard to the parents, nor with regard to his school and the law. The continuation, it was thus to release Tom from his guilt, to release him from the shame, to put back on his aggressors, to take time to speak about his physical experience, of sexuality and to answer his questions which were all the more naive as he had never spoken about that with his parents. I had to convince him to talk about it and not leave things as they were. I ask him the question:

"Is it possible to go back to school without saying so and without ensuring your safety? I don't think so. The boys who assaulted you must be punished and you must be protected.

Now, Tom wants to go back there but he also wants justice to be done, his aggressiveness testified to it from the first contact. He accepts that we speak about it with his mother, but asks me to say it without him to his father whom he fears, what I do not without pain but with a beautiful result. The father understands his educational and emotional mistake. He undertakes, in addition to speaking with his son and apologizing to him, to do everything possible to settle the case and protect him. The mobilization of the parents is completed by

1 - It's not that I don't want to, it's that I can't

that of the school which fully assures its task with the aggressors, their parents and punishes as it should. All of this allows Tom to return to school, anxiously at first, but, encouraged and valued, especially by his father, he takes his place, head held high.

This almost ideal outcome is unfortunately far from the rule. The school still has the unfortunate tendency to trivialize acts of aggression. The victim is not considered and sometimes forced to leave the school with a triple punishment: injustice, shame and exile. In the process, she loses her friends, her self-esteem and her dignity, preventing a harmonious psycho-affective development. Even if this outcome is positive for Tom, it will leave an indelible mark on him. It will be necessary to take care of its effects, in particular during adolescence, in his narcissistic, love and sexual development. The depreciation reflexes, the anxious background and the insecurity are sources of depressiveness. This is also true for racketeering, betrayals and humiliations from teachers and students, as well as for all traumatic situations, even if the seriousness of the consequences depends in part on the vulnerability and fragility of the child, his or her life context and family recourse. Parents must never trivialize these aggressions and, at the same time, not trap the child in a position of victim in front of all the others who would be villains. Narcissistic reinforcement by valuing their child must be combined with actions to protect him in social life, and therefore within the school itself.

Saying and doing: listening to your child before talking to him

If parents want to have a quality exchange with their child, they must first learn to listen to him/her, even if his/her words are disturbing, if they question education, if they complain about a lack of love or attention, if they appear to be in bad faith or very childish, even abusive in their criticism.

In this exchange, it is important to create a space for discussion that is close enough to confide in each other, but not so close as to violently intrude on the child's privacy. For example, it will be more productive to talk side by side while looking at the stars than while hugging your child. Cuddling is one time, free speech is often another.

In order to guarantee the quality of this exchange, it is necessary to know how to let the child speak, hold his tongue and respect the secrecy of what has been entrusted to him. If this has to be revealed in order to act in the child's interest because he or she is a victim of someone or something, in order to protect and defend him or her, it must be done in complete transparency with the child. Therefore, it is necessary to prepare him, to convince him of the merits of this approach. Otherwise, he will experience it as a betrayal.

If speech liberates, which is generally true, it is neither immediate nor systematic. Psychic elaboration and narcissistic repair are sometimes necessary before overcoming the anguish and the blockage in school and in relationships. The quality of the exchange is a factor of success of this psychic reconstruction which transforms the child-victim into a child-actor in his relationship with others.

I don't want to leave you

Lana, 13 years old, is consulting with her mother following a worrying information from the department's collection center, because she has been out of school without medical reason for three months. An immature young girl, she stares at her mother when I ask her questions. Is she afraid to speak or does she need her mother's permission? The latter invites her to tell me why she can no longer go to school after having, at first, refused the school bus and then the canteen, until she misses more and more classes and goes home to take refuge there. Her mother added that, seeing her so badly, she did not force her to go. Her attending physician had established a medical certificate of absence without specifying the date of resumption, hence this prolonged absence without further justification. At the beginning, her friend

I - It's not that I don't want to, it's that I can't

brought her lessons and homework but, as her mother did not push her, she did not start working. On her side, the mother has no job and spends most of the day in front of the television with her daughter. Both of them, curled up on the sofa, watch series, movies and reality shows. They don't see the time passing, as the mother explains to me to justify herself for not having fought against this deschooling, in fact a desocialization common to both of them.

I will learn more when I see Lana alone. Her anxiety tendencies increased during puberty. As a beautiful girl, boys would stick to her and make inappropriate sexual comments about her emerging femininity, as they often do. She felt harassed. She had anxious flashes and tried to escape from this situation for which she was not prepared, seeing herself as a little girl who just liked to share childish pleasures with her friends. It is because of this that, with her mother's agreement, she ran away from situations where abuse was not really controlled: the school bus and the canteen. The mother did not approach the school to complain and protect her daughter. When I am surprised, Lana explains that in fact there is not only harassment. The real problem, which worries her enormously, is her mother who is not well. That's why her mother didn't react. Lana doesn't want to leave her alone anymore, fearing that something bad will happen. That's why she stays with her, fearing that she won't see her when she comes back from college. The mother is becoming more and more alcoholic and depressive since her partner left her six months ago. Lana did not appreciate this man who humiliated her mother and did not hide from cheating on her. Moreover, she was afraid that he would bother her because he was also sticking to her. After the separation, she had been happy to be with her mother until this depression. This anxious school refusal was welcome, allowing her to take care of her mother and watch over her. The combination of these two motives, fleeing from being harassed because of her femininity and worrying about her depressed mother, explains the anxiety, the school refusal, but also the withdrawal of the mother-daughter couple in survival mode.

All of this led to a blockage linking unschooling and disinterest in school, reinforced by maternal apathy: mother without job, daughter without school. Lana ended up telling me: *I don't want to grow up, I want to stay with mom all the time,* a double entendre: I don't want to grow up because I don't want to be mistreated, I don't want to go through what my mother went through, and I would like to never leave her nor lose her, which I risk because she is not well.

I tell her what I understand, she answers: "*Being a woman, you don't realize it, it's a real pain.* I agree, because her words are right, and we agree to meet again. I suggest to her mother that she be treated by one of my colleagues, her daughter adding, in order to convince her, that if she doesn't go to school anymore, it's because she doesn't want to leave her for fear she'll commit suicide. This very mature statement by her daughter has a shocking effect on the mother who promises to get treatment as long as she returns to school, to which Lana intelligently replies that she will return to school when her mother has started treatment. We smile, we joke, it progresses.

In the following weeks, without activating a return to school because the summer vacations are coming, I focus on Lana's refusal, her fear of growing up, working with her on its multiple causes, including the rejection of her femininity linked to the hurtful attitude of the sexual harassment of the boys in her school, also linked to her perception of men, after having witnessed the humiliating and violent behavior of her mother's partner and having been afraid that he would also attack her. She refuses to become a young woman and makes sure not to show anything feminine until she neutralises herself in shabby clothes and tries to make herself ugly. She nibbles in front of the television without taking care of her body or even getting dressed. She wears old *leggings* with holes in them and a faded *sweatshirt,* even when she comes for a consultation. She has, she says to justify herself, put on a lot of weight, so her clothes don't fit her anymore. Obviously, the mother's carelessness rubs off on her. While the mother abuses alcohol and tobacco without eating, she becomes bulimic. I alert them, because they must

1 - It's not that I don't want to, it's that I can't

be aware of this disturbing slide, saying that they are captives and that by way of taking care of themselves they both plunge into isolation and go towards their perdition.

Dreading the social services investigation that is looming as a result of the report, the mother has finally started treatment while Lana decides to return to school even before the vacations, but she is very scared. Reassured to see her mother react, she calmed down and came to her senses. She sees the extent of the damage: her young teenage body has become shapeless in her eyes. I prefer to exempt her from a too early recovery so that everything can happen in good conditions. Indeed, for the moment, psychotherapy has not allowed her to regain her self-confidence nor the capacity to face relationships within the school. Visibly relieved, she took a new step by explaining that her father had left when she was only 3 months old. She didn't know anything about him, her mother never talked about him. Lana didn't dare ask questions for fear of hurting her feelings and making her sad. *I would just like to know who he is, but not to meet him, especially since he must be as bad a man as the others.* She fears him because she sees her mother as a woman who has always been mistreated by men. She adds: *I would like to have a father like you, who listens to me, who protects me and who wants me to respect myself,* a statement that marks a strong moment in the psychotherapy and its narcissistic support.

It took all this time before Lana could bring up the issue of her father. She began by taking care of her pillar, her mother, unable to do so on her own, so as not to lose the one person who was supposed to protect her. Her de-schooling allowed her to stay with her, captive while believing she was caring. She became aware of the argument of her refusal to grow up, sensible and justified, so as not to become the object of harassment by the teenagers at school but also so as not to leave her mother. The real reason is that in fact her psychic construction was in search of a protective model in order to guide her in her development as a woman, in her social and psycho-affective relationships. It was not with her mother's ex-partner nor with her family, scattered and dislocated by conflicts, that she could find it. Having understood this through therapeutic transference, she timidly allowed herself to criticize her mother's attitude, who had deprived her of a father and, worse, had never told her anything about this father.

Protecting her mother was a reactionary formation to keep the resentment and aggression she unknowingly felt toward her from showing through. She was able to express her ambivalence towards her mother in psychotherapy. Without blaming her for it, she was able to measure her failure and her egocentricity. With my help, she finally demanded that her mother tell her in my presence who her father was, what she knew about him, and asked for permission to contact him, while making it clear that this was not a betrayal of her and certainly not a fathering of her, since he had abandoned her. Lana took advantage of the vacations to seek this father and, as it is unfortunately often the case, she found herself in front of a man who had remade his life. If he accepted to meet her, the current did not pass between them. She did not seek to see him again, but, proud and appeased to have taken the step, she was able to take care of herself again, to get dressed, to make herself beautiful, to assert herself in front of her mother who was better thanks to the psychiatric follow-up. She also reconnected with a cousin.

At the end of her commitment and efforts, she felt able to face the gaze of the other students, whom she now saw as rough-edged teenagers. She knew that she would not be taken in by men, that she would not follow her mother's path, but she still planned to meet *a smart boy* one day. The social inquiry didn't have time to set in and she was already back in school.

Saying and doing: beware, one cause can hide another

If the reason put forward (for Lana, sexual and sexist school harassment) is important because of its traumatic dimension, it can always hide another reason. In order to be effective in their support, the parents and the psychologist must always keep in mind the complexity of the situations.

1 - It's not that I don't want to, it's that I can't

If the help brought is limited to a technique to reinforce the ego and its defenses by a kind of psycho-education, the risk is to remain deaf to the difficulty to build oneself inherent to an emotional disorder sometimes very buried. This disorder cannot be solved with advice or re-education of parasitic thoughts.

Parents and professionals must take the time to listen and insist on discovering what is hidden behind what is seen and shown. Anxious school refusal is a symptom, a call and a suffering. This forces us to identify and treat the crisis in depth, often caught in an inner duality. Without this effort to deepen the causality, the risk is to compromise the child's life and success in the long term.

Going back to school does not mean that all problems are solved. Of course, it is a happy stage, but only a stage. It is better to remain attentive, to listen, and to continue the care undertaken until the anxiety disappears and the appeasement is confirmed.

I'm afraid you won't come looking for me

One month after entering the first grade, Jules, 6 years old, could not get through the school door. The parents say they have tried everything with the supportive help of the teacher, consoling him, reassuring him with gentleness then firmness. Nothing works, Jules clings to his parents, whether it is the father or the mother who accompanies him. He cries and struggles, even more so if he is carried into the classroom. Unlike other frightened children, nothing can calm him down, the parents have to take him home. The situation is blocked, so he stays with his nanny, who is available and warm. During the consultation, I learn that the parents really forgot him once at the school exit. The teacher was getting impatient and they arrived half an hour late. A moment of tension, the teacher raised his voice because they had the annoying habit of picking up their child as late as possible. Panicked, Jules was consoled by his mother who promised never to do it again. Is this a reason to cause such a blockage? How many children are forgotten at the end of school and, if they keep a trace of anxiety, is it a trauma? This does not prevent them from returning to school. I continue my investigation and explore the context of this school block with anxiety.

The problem is that the parents come to the consultation with Jules' little brother, 2 years old, who gets their full attention in the waiting room. They want to go into the office with him and are surprised that I object, telling them that this only concerns Jules and them, but not the little brother. The father stays in the waiting room while I receive Jules and his mother. She tells me that they did everything to reassure him, apologized, bought him a new stuffed animal to add to the many others already on his bed. The mother is sorry and feels guilty. She adds that they had their son late and are badly organized, but they love him very much. Since the nursery, she recognizes that they are often the last to take Jules back, aware that it is not good for him, especially since this year there is the stress of the first grade and the demands of the teacher who, according to Jules, is strict. For her, he is a good teacher, rather *cool*. I ask Jules who confirms:

"He's nice, but he yells if we don't do it right.

He adds:

- I'm a little afraid with him, afraid I won't make it.

The mother adds:

- Besides, you have to sit still and Jules can't do that.

He nods while fidgeting more and more in the chair as his mother describes his situation.

Jules starts to be interested in our discussion when we mention the place occupied by the little brother, a little invasive according to the mother, who adds:

- Jules is more sensitive since the birth of the little one, more sensitive, while there is no reason, we do everything the same for both of them, and we love them both very much, right Jules?

He grimaces, I take the opportunity to give him the floor, he dares to say:

1 - It's not that I don't want to, it's that I can't

- He's boring.

Black look of his mother, I temporize, she recognizes:

- It's true that sometimes it's a bit annoying, it takes up a lot of space, but you're looking for it too.

I insist to Jules:

- It's true that the little ones are often like that, especially when the parents say that the big one must set an example and be nice to the little one because he doesn't realize what he's doing.

We understand each other, he smiles and strengthens himself by telling what the little one is doing to him:

- He hits me, he takes my toys. When I take them back, he starts crying and I get caught.

The mother responds:

- You're exaggerating, you're not soft on him either.

I add:

- He probably has his reasons for not being soft on him.

Mother:

- You're right, I thought about it; what he went through when his brother was born must not have been very joyful. He was even more upset because we moved at the same time. His father rushed him to his grandparents' house when I entered the clinic. The childbirth being complicated, he stayed there for ten days. When he came back, we were already in the new house. We had made a nice room for him, didn't we, my doudou? but he must not have understood what was happening to him. We had no choice but to do it. Do you understand that, sweetie?

To which he replies:

- I liked my old house and my little school better. Why did you change everything? I don't have my friends anymore. I never wanted a little brother.

There follows a dialogue between mother and son during which I do not intervene. She explains, reassures, tells him that she loves him more than anything... while Jules insists on his nostalgia, obviously enjoying being caressed by his mother's words. I speak up:

- Well, here it is, all this had to be said, the little intruder, the new house, that makes a lot especially when one does not understand what happens. One is abandoned, a little like the Little Thumb. When you come back, you are always afraid to be abandoned and you are a little bit angry, it's normal, your parents made you a funny joke and they didn't think to explain you all that.

The mother adds:

- He was very sweet with his little brother, we didn't realize that he might be sad. We just thought he was a little shy.

Segueing:

- I believe that Jules had a small depression. Since he didn't say anything, it set in, with the feeling of being abandoned and the fear of being abandoned again, especially since his parents came to get him last, which didn't help.

Jules kisses his mother who hugs him tightly. I add:

- Well, Jules, since your dad isn't here, you'll explain to him what we talked about, he needs to understand."

It would be necessary to relate in detail this long resolutive interview to understand its importance. We unraveled the family history to get to the core of the anguish, and then began to weave a solid relationship through words, hugs and caresses between Jules and his mother. This was the prerequisite for the return to an inner security before the birth of the little brother. Often, because of embarrassment, denial, trivialization or fear of accentuating the malaise, this is not said, is not thought of, or is thought of very little because *we love each other, there is no problem*. It is not a question of a lack of love but of reference points and pillars to build one's inner security in order to be able to face new situations without the anguish of abandonment or the fear of rejection. Self-confidence is built on confidence in others, above all in the parents. Therefore, if the equivalent of abandonment (forgetfulness at school, impression of disinterest...) punctuates the path and the trials that the children must face - this was the case for Jules even if for the parents it was only a problem of organization -, it will be the confirmation for the

1 - It's not that I don't want to, it's that I can't

child of the risk of not seeing his parents again, of being alone in the world, convinced of being unloved in favor of a younger child. During psychotherapy for school phobia, it often happens that children express this form of anguish which is difficult for parents to decipher. The child expresses his feelings and sensations with the words he has at his disposal. Parents may not understand him, find him unfair, in bad faith when he says, as I often hear: *Every time, I am the one who gets punished, he, you never see what he does to me. If he starts, then I hit him,* or: *He always has gifts and I never have anything.* Of course, it can be a child who wants to take up all the space, to leave nothing to the other, refuses to share, nostalgia for a unique time as a child, but it can also be a feeling of abandonment based on clumsiness for which the parents do not have to feel guilty. They only have to be aware that their child has, as a result, the impression that he or she does not count for them. This is aggravated by the educational obligation to point out and repress deviant behaviors and the opposition of the child who has found only this behavior to express his complaint, his aggressiveness until sometimes staging a suicidal equivalent. In general, this works, the parents are panicked and give in to the educational dimension in front of the threat. This allows the child to arouse interest and thus perverts the affective relationship.

Confident, Jules talks about his new school where he doesn't know anyone and where he can't make any friends. He stays in his corner, sad, and thinks about his parents who miss him. He adds that if someone would play with him, he would not think about it. During our interviews, I realize that he doesn't have the instructions to get in touch with others. His shyness prevents him from doing so, he isolates himself, which maintains his malaise and the anxious wait to return home.

This will be the second phase of the psychotherapy, guiding him with the help of the parents towards confidence in his abilities, resources and creativity in shared initiatives and activities. In the meantime, thanks to the attention of his mother and father, he managed to return to school. The parents promised that they would never again come late, or, in case of force majeure, they would warn the teacher so that Jules would not worry. The mother set up a symbolic link with him, a doudou-relay, a small object slipped into his pencil case, always at his disposal, a sort of code at a distance that secures their relationship. The father told him about the difficulties he had had, also shy, in making friends at his age. Together they looked for solutions, which was enough for Jules to reach out to other students, to make friends and to consolidate his relationships by inviting them to his birthday party. As for the little brother, he was gently brought to heel so as not to encroach on Jules' world, especially his toys and his room.

Saying and doing: hearing and resolving feelings of abandonment

The feeling of abandonment cannot be reasoned with. It crosses the body, like a tear, an emptiness which digs itself in the heart of the being. To feel the anxiety of abandonment is a real trauma, and therefore each situation that reminds us of it, from near or far, awakens an anxiety-signal. Many children express this through school phobia.

Not only must it be taken seriously, but reassurance is not enough. It is necessary to support the child's reference points, to ensure and reinforce the emotional security that protects him and allows him to build his inner security and his capacity to face separations.

The child is better when he starts to boast and tries to test his parents to prove their love for him. He becomes a little aggressive, cumbersome, but this is the sign of the exit from the malaise and the self-confidence that is being forged. Some parents complain about it, they are not used to their child looking for them, in the sense of asking more and provoking them. They have to deal with this stage, gently and without giving up their education but avoiding what can be interpreted by the child as a rejection, a devaluation. It is a convalescence that requires precautions to avoid a relapse, which is often more difficult to overcome.

It is desirable, if possible, that the teacher and the school administration be involved in this recovery: to give the child confidence, to give

I - It's not that I don't want to, it's that I can't

him responsibilities in the classroom and to facilitate the relationship with others through games and shared work. Be careful with words that can hurt, the child is attentive to them.

If these conditions are not met, the result is a residual anxiety that can be disabling, with relational inhibition, attention and memory problems, and learning difficulties, including certain forms of dyslexia and dyspraxia if the school phobia is very early. Sometimes, the phobia evolves quietly, hidden in a withdrawal. This tends to activate school harassment by students or clumsy teachers who take advantage of the child's vulnerability by masking their distress, including from their parents. Some so-called neurodevelopmental disorders are in fact an early depressive anxiety that goes unnoticed.

After an episode of school phobia linked to separation anxiety, parents must remain vigilant in their concern for their child but also in the way he/she is treated at school. The attention of the teacher and the transitional arrangement of the reception is essential but must not lead to a "handicap" label and stigmatizing measures.

They made me ashamed

Parents, professionals, let's always remain vigilant because appearances are deceiving. I receive a 13 year old pre-teen girl, visibly in rebellion. She is accompanied by her parents, who are confused, and who tell us about the unbearable situation she puts them through. If they are aware that she is suffering, they do not understand why.

"She hasn't been to school for ten months and doesn't eat, she has lost 5 kg since last year, she scarifies herself, she threatens to commit suicide, she rejects her sister, she attacks us. She even raised her hand on me, says the mother.

- We want to help her but she refuses to talk, she screams, slams the doors and isolates herself in her room. I hear her crying and when I come to talk to her, she sends me away. She doesn't sleep at night and neither do I, I'm very afraid she'll do something stupid," says the father.

- She has not been in school since the second quarter of 6th grade. We hoped she would start again in the first semester of 5th grade. She lasted ten days, we believed in it, but she dropped out and doesn't want to go back. If I insist, she insults me," adds the mother.

While the parents explain the situation with the necessary tact because they know that their daughter can go off at any moment, I observe her, sad and frowning. She is there against her will and has told her parents that she won't talk, that she doesn't care. She is dressed all in black, gothic style, with mittens and long sleeves that hide her scarification marks. She glares at us. The tension, at its peak, rose as the parents described the long crisis they are going through, adding that they are exhausted. Predictably, she explodes:

- Stop! Stop or I'm out of here. You don't understand anything anyway. You're the ones who suck, you didn't even see how bad I was, and even in primary school I was embarrassed. They were all against me, you too, and Julie. Yes, I know I suck but that's not a reason.

Father tempers:

- Why you didn't tell us, we can't guess. To us, you were fine. You know you don't suck, you just have some difficulties in French.

- That's it, keep going! You're the worst, you call me a bum, you say I'm no good, I'll never amount to anything, so stop it or I'm gone!

I ask her if she wants to talk alone with me and the answer is not long in coming:

- You, don't mess with me, I'm not crazy, I have nothing to do here.

She leaves the office violently and runs out into the street. The father joins her and I continue to speak with the mother, in tears, who feels guilty for not having seen it coming:

- It's true that she has difficulties, it all started in fourth grade. She was diagnosed as dyslexic and dysgraphic. We did what was necessary, she took speech therapy. Homework went on for hours, as if she didn't want to understand anything. She would get stuck and it always ended badly. We did not do it very well, but in those moments, words are more important than thoughts. It's true, her father was a bit hard

I - It's not that I don't want to, it's that I can't

on her. He is like that, you can't change him. We couldn't cope with her. We weren't used to it because her sister Julie was never a problem, she's brilliant. I recognize that it must be difficult for Prune. She is always comparing herself to her sister who is doing everything right and who is not always nice to her. It's like they hate each other... deep down, I'm sure they like each other. In any case, if she was harassed, we didn't see anything and she never told us.

I add:

- It's no wonder, you see, she devalues and mistreats herself. She must be ashamed of herself, which is not new. I'm going to see her again as soon as I can, she's really in pain."

We make an appointment, as a challenge against her refusal that I thought I heard as a call for help.

Prune comes alone, I am surprised.

"My parents are waiting in the car, it's better, I prefer, I don't want them to hear what I have to tell you.

Obviously, she is determined to speak and seems to have prepared what she has to say. She begins:

-I was so ashamed that I never said anything to my parents. What I experienced in elementary school was really horrible. They were all against me, humiliating me. It started with my first name: "You're a plum, you look like a plum", then it was my name that sounds like the sidewalk, the boys called me a whore, they pulled down my panties and touched me. I was a little fat, so they called me "the fat, sucking plum." I never dared to tell my parents about it, especially my father who told me I was fat. You heard, the last time they talked about my sister Julie, their little darling. Well, she calls me Bécassine. They don't know that, she does it behind their backs, so I get angry and then I take the blame. Anyway, they only believe her. They think I'm a bad person, they don't want to understand. You know, their dyslexia story is bullshit. I was so blocked that I couldn't even write and think. I was always afraid I was going to get it wrong, I would get really mad, like panic. I couldn't even read anymore. I was ashamed! Fortunately, my speech therapist was really nice, she understood, she helped me a lot. She was the only one who gave me back my confidence. With her, I was relaxed and I wrote well, but at school and at home, it was a disaster. She told me that I was normal, that I was just very scared. My parents didn't want to know and didn't believe her. They don't trust me anyway. I don't want to stay at home anymore.

Prune is silent. She cries, I speak again:

- You know, what you went through in school was a real trauma. On top of that, you had no support. Harassment destroys you, makes you feel ashamed of yourself, makes you withdraw and lose your abilities. You can't do anything anymore, as you said, you feel like you're at fault, like you're a nobody. It's an infernal spiral, the more you are bothered, the more you are humiliated, the more you are ashamed, it's like that until you want to destroy yourself by attacking your body that you hate because you have been humiliated and because someone has dared to touch you, to dirty you. Even if they tell you that you are beautiful, that you are intelligent, you can't believe it because you only see yourself through the eyes of those who have traumatized you. You see, it's sad, you even end up wanting to end your life. That's what happens to all the people who are traumatized by the abuse of others who deserve to be condemned for what they do. If you can't talk about it, you can't get through it on your own. I agree with you, your parents don't get it. I thank you for trusting me, I will do everything I can to help you."

As trust has begun to be established with Prune, I make it clear to the parents that, for a while, they must stay away from the psychotherapy. Indeed, I am all the more bound to secrecy since their daughter is on pins and needles because they have been clumsy, even if their intentions were not bad. I ask them to remain attentive and supportive, to ask Julie to do the same, making her understand that her sister is in danger. They have my promise that if their behavior changes and Prune realizes it, we can talk to each other and to her again. They agree, and this will help their daughter, who has severe depression associated

I - It's not that I don't want to, it's that I can't

with post-traumatic stress disorder dating back to elementary school. The symptoms of self-destruction and cognitive disorders, including the alleged dyslexia, not validated by the speech therapist who also and above all played a role of psychological support, enter into this traumatic context, including on the part of the deaf and blind parents to the malaise of their daughter, particularly the father who accentuated the devaluation. Aware of the infernal spiral in which they have entered, they too make great efforts and show commitment to restore a relationship of trust with their daughter.

After this first step where Prune was able to express her suffering and her desperate rage, I asked her to tell me in detail what she had experienced since the third grade, both at school and with her sister and her parents. As we know, the majority of school phobias today are linked to separation anxiety in young children and to harassment in all its forms, especially in middle school. For Prune, and this is often the case with young children whose violence and nastiness we don't want to see unless we witness it live, the harassment started very early. In her case, the effects are frightening because they affect the first school learning, the discovery of the image of the body through the glance of the others and the narcissistic consolidation which will make it possible to face the obstacles without living them like failures. Prune gives reason to those who humiliate her and even adds to it: *I am ugly, I am fat, I am stupid, I am null. And I can't even make friends. Each time, they move away or betray me.* This is what she believed, and so far no one has been able to convince her otherwise, because even her parents, annoyed by her inhibition and opposition to school work, told her that she would never amount to anything, that she was a loser, and worse, they compared her to her sister, who was obviously devoid of empathy and toxic, too. This is Prune's sad observation, and also a call for help, as with the speech therapist. How could she put up with all this? She explains to me the only solution she has found:

"Since I couldn't do it, I didn't make any more effort. In fourth grade, it was horrible. I dropped everything and I was relieved to know that

I was repeating, so I wouldn't have to put up with them anymore. So I had a little respite but when I got to 6th grade, it started all over again with the same people, I was the big cow, I was stupid, I was a *loser*, they said I didn't belong here, that I should go to the SEGPA and a lot of other things that I don't even dare to tell you because it was so disgusting.

Isolated, once again humiliated, including by other students joining the primary school gang, she could not stand it. That's when the scarifications started, the suicidal ideas, but above all an anguish that took her in the stomach all the time, in the evening, in the morning and at night with nightmares of pursuit and others where she killed everyone, including her family. Her rebelliousness and great aggressiveness helped her to externalize her rage and despair and allowed her not to commit suicide. But it was not far off, as is sadly the case for many young adolescents who, in these situations, can suddenly commit suicide.

One day, having heard that a young American boy had gone on a rampage at his school where he had experienced terrible bullying, she said to me:

"If I listened to myself, I would do what he did. I'd come into the classroom with my *Kalash* and kill them all, even the teachers, who didn't want to see when I was being insulted. While I'm at it, I'd do the same to my sister, just like that, in peace! My parents, maybe not, I need them, even if they suck.

To which I reply:

- I understand you, it's better to think that than to commit suicide, but fortunately there are other solutions, because then you would end up in prison and that would be even worse. We'll look for other solutions."

This is the final therapeutic step. Rather than withdrawing, rather than acting out, I suggest that Prune transform her rage into a conquest of herself, of her value, of her abilities and creativity, which has already translated into her style of dress and her ability to express herself. This becomes her fight against the self-destructive forces that have only taken on the attacks from students, teachers, her sister and her parents.

I - It's not that I don't want to, it's that I can't

Prune takes it as a revenge, which is radically different from revenge. We can finally look together for what will help her.

First decision, no more help or control of school work by the parents, except at his request. Instead, regular help from a tutor. She knows who to suggest to her parents. Second decision, she will enroll in a *hip-hop* class, which she is afraid to do but very much wants to do. Third decision, she will not go back to the school she hates and that embodies her destruction. She decided this, and I added that she could start at another college after Christmas break. This gives her two months to prepare and strengthen herself. Fourth, she doesn't want to make a fuss at school or press charges because she doesn't want to *stir up trouble* and risk getting hurt. She prefers to turn to a new stage of life, even if she knows that it is not forgotten and that maybe, one day, she will find the way to denounce it. *It would be worse, I prefer not to see them anymore and to move on,* which says the fear of her harassers and the hold they still have on her, which will be the case until she succeeds, thanks to her life experiences, in consolidating a valuation of herself.

It remains to make the parents understand and accept this. Prune chooses to talk to them in my presence and with my support. In a family discussion, we go over all the important elements of the psychotherapy, taking care of the limits of secrecy, and then dictate the proposals which are very well accepted by the parents, even if they would have liked to question the college, or even to file a complaint, which they consider, like me, legitimate. We agree that it will always be possible to do it later on at Prune's request. If the parents accept these proposals, it is because they have worked to make their daughter feel more comfortable. Relationships have clearly improved, and if Prune puts color in her style, it is, says the mother, since the two sisters went shopping together: "I gave them free time and they warmed the credit card. They came back happy and delighted. It's a real pleasure for us.

After these two months of taking care of her body and psyche, without any imposed school work, Prune, who had nevertheless opened her books, was ready to enter her new school after having verified that she was going *incognito*. As a tutor, she had chosen a former teacher, her neighbor, the only one who, she said, understood and supported her. Hairdresser, beautician for her acne, check-up with the attending physician and even nails, everything was done with the support and warm complicity of her mother and sister.

End of the school year: Prune seems to have rebuilt herself well, notably on the cognitive level with an improvement in her school results, and on the narcissistic level with a self-esteem that, even if she remains fragile, is on the right track to rebuild herself. Everyone is vigilant so that she does not experience the slightest situation of mistreatment, the school being warned and especially Prune knowing how to defend herself and be respected. As for the scarifications, it is difficult to give them up because they have become very addictive but, after a year, she is beginning to manage them even if the desire and the need, as with drugs, are still there.

Saying and doing: helping him to repair himself after a harassment

If a child's behavior changes - withdrawal, aggressiveness, decrease in interest and school results, sadness, loss of vital impetus - one should always think of a school bullying situation because it is frequent and causes many anxious school refusals. Being vigilant and reacting quickly, whether the school likes it or not, is the best way to prevent school phobia linked to mistreatment by students or teachers.

Questions that are too direct and frontal have the effect of keeping the child silent. It is better to assume that the child does not know what is happening to him or her, that he or she feels guilty and ashamed to talk about it. Empathetic communication of our intuitions about the cause of the malaise can open the door to his confidences, provided that the moment is well chosen, in a calm environment, without witnesses and with the guarantee of a well-kept secret.

The attacks on the body - scarification and self-mutilation - are only an expression of the great suffering that cuts into the heart and body of the being. Faced with this, getting carried away can only

I - It's not that I don't want to, it's that I can't

make the situation worse. Appealing to reason is useless. There is just to take care of the bruised body to try to repair the evil thanks to a real and emotional bandage, thanks to a form of consolation of the wounded being.

In helping the child, it is important to be in tune with what he or she is willing to do to fight the harassment. Suddenly intervening at school or filing a complaint without the child being ready to do so can put him or her in a delicate situation that aggravates his or her anxiety, even if the threat of reprisals should not dictate cowardice in the actions to be taken. This does not mean that nothing should be done, but that it should be done with tact and the child's agreement.

If starting again from scratch, opening a new page, is an illusion because the psychological wound cannot be healed with a wave of a magic wand, it is essential to do everything possible to achieve this. There is no point in changing schools, cutting toxic links and closing social networks if this is not proposed at the same time as engaging in intensive psychotherapy for the child, coupled if necessary with family therapy.

A situation of school phobia linked to bullying, whatever it may be, requires attention to the child's psychological and cognitive evolution until the end of adolescence, in order to ensure that the repair is not just a band-aid on a wound that has remained open. Parents must ensure that their child is valued and narcissistically reinforced in order to guarantee a true reconstruction of the child's psyche.

II - It's okay, I'll stop, I don't want any more!

School absenteeism in adolescence is both considerable and worrying. Although it affects all fields of study, it is much more important in vocational sections than in general and technological sections. It has increased during the pandemic. Approximately 100,000 students are gradually dropping out of school, and this starts very early in the year, as early as the All Saints' Day vacations. The dropout figures have not improved despite the initiatives taken by the National Education System to curb the phenomenon. In fact, they have tended to increase since the disruption caused by the pandemic and the lockdown. These data concern the emerging part of the population of young people in serious difficulty at school for various reasons: at least one and a half million according to the 2021 evaluation by the OpinionWay education barometer[1] , especially boys, whose absenteeism and dropout rate are higher. What do they say? *If you miss school once, it's easy after that, you quickly get used to it, especially if you don't keep up, you drop out, you get even more bored, and you end up not going.* How many times have I heard this kind of talk from teenagers who add: *"Even if I'm forced,*

---

1. https://etudiant.lefigaro.fr/article/selon-un-sondage-le-decrochage-scolaire-atteint-un-pic-au-moment-des-vacances-de-la-toussaint_d7d793cc-2cd5-11ec-81bc-f04a2133736d/

I don't want to go anymore. There's nothing you can do about it, I don't care about school anymore, and it's too late anyway. All this is said in a language that is often more flowery!

This slide from absenteeism to dropping out and then to dropping out of school through refusal in the form of inertia or opposition leaves parents disoriented and powerless in the face of their child's resistance. As for the teachers and the school administration, for reasons that are partly justified, they are so discredited in the eyes of these young people that they no longer have any positive impact on them, despite efforts to bring them back to school or to offer them more appropriate training.

The problem, as we will see in this second part, is that this dropout is occurring earlier and earlier, and concerns young people in middle school, as early as 13 or 14 years old. Sometimes all it takes is a good listening ear and personalized measures to re-establish contact and the desire to learn, but the older the dropout, the less constructive the proposals made to him or her.

It's useless, it's useless

I see a teenager, 15 years old, following a violent altercation with his father, who is devastated that he has come to blows with his son and that his son has reacted violently by hitting him. Both regret having come to this end. They don't understand each other, they don't talk to each other and the situation is stuck. When he is at home, Nathan isolates himself in his room, with his phone, video games and headphones on. He doesn't answer his parents' calls, either in the morning to get him off to school or for meals. In the late afternoon, he goes out and joins his friends to play soccer and other distractions. The parents don't know what he's been up to when he comes home at 11 p.m. to spend part of the night on his screens. He still asks his parents to sleep over at a friend's house, but if they refuse he goes anyway, sometimes for an entire weekend. The father laments that he has no authority or educational control over his son, who nods and adds: "Get *used to it, that's what teenagers are like*. Nathan lives his life the way he wants to and doesn't suffer from anything. If he agrees to meet me, it is to appease his father, more out of opportunism than empathy. Indeed, the father having hardened his condition at home, he is disturbed in his comfort. He tries to be seductive with me, probably hoping that I will interfere in his favor. Aside from this altercation, he is not aggressive or delinquent, he just wants to be allowed to do what he wants when he wants. He doesn't have a plan, nor the desire to seek one.

I receive him alone. He explains to me that his parents work a lot, that he does not want to follow their example. He wants to enjoy his youth: "*I'm not into work*. Alone at home, he is quiet and does what he likes. It annoys him when his studious younger sister comes home from school. When he sees her working, it makes him a little uncomfortable. I ask, he answers:

"She's lucky, it's too easy for her, she's a nerd, she's the opposite of me.

He seems a little moved. I take the opportunity to ask him to tell me about his school career.

- In elementary school, things were going well, I was pretty good. In 6th grade, my parents put me in a private school because they were working a lot. They didn't have time to keep up with me. I didn't work very hard, so that was the only solution they could come up with. The problem was that I had no friends and the teachers were backward. I couldn't accept that they talked to me like I was a moron, so I messed up and got kicked out at the end of 6th grade. After that, I went to my local school but I didn't feel like working anymore, I preferred to laugh with my friends that I had found again. That's when I dropped out, they had broken me so much before, the private teachers, that I was disgusted with school. I started not to go anymore. My parents didn't know anything, I would leave in the morning and go for a walk in the city with a friend who did the same thing. Dad found out, got mad and took everything away from me. He didn't want to know why

II - It's okay, I'll stop, I don't want any more!

I didn't go anymore. For him, school was a place where you went and kept your mouth shut.

Nathan's story provides insight into how the school dropout began. It started with a slide, for the reasons he describes, until he was completely out of school for over a year. Because he was no longer working, his grades were falling. The more he was absent, the less he understood, and therefore the more bored he became. It's a downward spiral that people describe when they start to drop out. It goes very fast and it is difficult for them to go back, to get back into school. Criticism and sanctions from the school come thick and fast, which only adds to their rejection of school. As for the parents, after having tried to help him, they became discouraged and also tried unsuccessfully to impose sanctions. At some point, the high school imposed a reorientation that he underwent. Refusing and not knowing how to project himself beyond the present, he is directed towards a pre-pro class in order to awaken a professional orientation. Out of spite, hoping that he would invest himself in it, he was directed towards the health sector. As it was foreseeable, he does not provide any work and, very quickly, does not go to school anymore. The situation is stuck. He knows what he doesn't want: school, but he doesn't want to know what else is on the horizon. What are *they all doing messing with my head, I want to be let go*, he says, paradoxically angry, which indicates a discomfort in his escape.

During our interviews, while I was careful not to judge his attitude or want him to return to high school at any cost, he provided valuable insights to help him. His success in elementary school indicates that he has no deficits, neither intellectual, instrumental, nor cognitive. He was devalued by teachers who were clumsy, to say the least, without recourse, alone in his class and at odds with his parents who imposed this strict private school on him. He does not speak to them, isolates himself, settles into an oppositional inertia of a je-m'en-foutiste nature, which goes unnoticed, and a behaviour of failure which allows him to go where he should have been, in his local college with his friends. It is there that he externalizes his opposition at the same time as he finds adolescent pleasures and distractions. But the period in the private school, which was trying, made him lose confidence in his abilities and led him to disinvest in school learning without realizing that he was suffering because of the devaluation. Unconsciously, he no longer wants to take the risk of failure and be humiliated by it. Laughing and escaping from school work have a restorative effect, but the loop closes against him: he is punished for his lack of work and his behavior deemed unacceptable. Absenteeism is his response, one that gradually leads him to a fatal dropout. He is not indifferent to his sister's success, as witnessed by his suffering masked by his je-m'en-foutiste attitude, his lack of desire and his refusal to project himself. He obviously defends himself against a depressive depreciation. For all that, he does not do anything, does not fall into delinquency, which augurs well for the possibility of a good evolution, but under what conditions?

This is where the rebuilding of self-esteem and confidence in one's abilities comes in. There is no point in convincing them of this, they need to have a concrete experience that makes them want to get back into a life project and regain their confidence. He tried unsuccessfully to get into a micro-high school, which was very accommodating, and had no concrete contact with the Compagnons du devoir because the rules were strict, obviously too strict in his eyes. Finally, it was a friend of the parents, a winegrower, who offered him a solution. The father did not see a future as a wine worker for his son, but he refrained from any criticism, which saved the project. Nathan enjoyed the simple and repetitive work in the vineyard. Rather courageous, he gradually took initiative and became interested in the running of the business. The excellent relationship with his internship boss, who was ready to teach him the secrets of wine making, consolidated his choice of this path. Thanks to this, he was able to get back into teaching by doing a work-study program in an oenology and viticulture establishment. The return to a school was delicate, but alternating between work

II - It's okay, I'll stop, I don't want any more!

and concrete teaching in the field he learned to love allowed him to succeed in his studies and to project himself into his professional life. Without the empathetic, positive help of the winemaker, he would have evolved like many dropouts who do not *find* themselves. They live off their parents and then society. They often evolve towards petty crime, with no joyful perspective for their lives, with a depressive background and frequent addictive toxic behaviors that aggravate their escape and social failure.

Saying and doing: how do you overcome a school dropout?

Can he hang up? is the agonizing question that parents of teenage dropouts ask themselves. To do this, they must deal with three essential facts:

*The pedagogy, that of the parents and the school being very often compromised, it is necessary to turn to original solutions, such as that of Nathan.

*Desire, because even if it seems that the young dropout is carefree and happy, deep down it is often the opposite. They forbid themselves to project themselves. Desire is paralyzed or diluted in distractive occupation so as not to think and especially not to anticipate anything.

*Authority, because if, at first, it fails to impose reschooling, with the effect of accentuating passive or aggressive opposition, then it becomes essential, implicitly requested by the adolescent if an interesting path is offered to him. Whether it is a question of a personalized pedagogical approach or an original pathway: the companions of duty who save dropouts in spite of or thanks to their strong demands, a master of training in a demanding profession, who transmits it by giving the desire to do so with firmness and empathy, which is not given to every boss who shows authority.

We must not put the cart before the horse, which means that the primary goal is not to get the young person back into school at all costs, but to determine where, when and how the dropout occurred. This implies a quality of exchange with the teenager to enable him or her to get out of the trap, even more so if it is comfortable. The family approach, parental guidance, psychotherapy with the teenager, is the whole package that must be offered to understand the impasse, unblock the school refusal, rehabilitate the life project and, in short, restore confidence and positive values to the young person and his family.

In order to get out of the dropout situation, life at home and outside must not be too comfortable and must not allow the illusion of the always-present-happy to take hold. Well-tempered authority is a factor in awakening desire. It makes it possible to reorganize a living environment, whether the teenager likes it or not, but in his or her interest. We must not lose sight of the fact that they must try a constructive experience. In order to make him/her decide, it is necessary to be solid and warm in the face of his/her resistance, whether it is passive or aggressive. And if possible, show originality, off the beaten track.

Finally, it must be recognized today that since compulsory schooling goes up to 16 years of age and compulsory work up to 18 years of age, some children and adolescents have great difficulty in dealing with the abstraction of teaching and its pedagogy. The insistence and rigidity of the normative system, the deliberate or clumsy humiliation of teachers, the too early and imposed orientations, the exclusion in the underhanded forms of devalued courses of study: all this incites pupils in difficulty to absenteeism, to drop out and to fail. The National Education still refuses to accept pedagogical methods based on concrete and truly participative projects, on the sharing of experience and on real but self-managed authority within the group of students. If Freinet and related methods have proved their worth in helping young people succeed and reducing school dropout, why not develop them further and step up the effort put into, for example, micro-schools and second-chance schools (see the chapter on schooling support systems, paragraph "Other arrangements").

II - It's okay, I'll stop, I don't want any more!

I'm bored, school is not for me

I don't mind coming to see you. If it makes my parents happy, I'll do it… you know, I'm not crazy or abnormal, I just don't want to go to school anymore. Eliott, 12 years old, explains to me calmly that he is coming because he hasn't been going to school for several months, considering that he doesn't learn anything, that the students are immature and only think about soccer and video games, which doesn't interest him. His parents add that he has high intellectual potential, confirmed by an IQ test taken when he was in third grade. They accept the idea that Eliott is bored because he has no academic difficulties despite having skipped the fourth grade, and that his favorite occupations do not correspond to those of the other students or to the education offered by the school. He is passionate about astronomy. His extraordinary scientific culture does not prevent him from being interested in politics. In other words, he doesn't find his place in a school like his, even if it's a good one. Aware of his problem, the teachers proposed a very flexible individualized reception project whose aim was to ensure that he did not cut himself off from social relations in school life, that he followed the program more or less so as not to compromise his future and his university studies, but also that he conformed to the rules of the establishment. Despite these arrangements, Eliott did not return to school and only worked on the subjects that interested him, alone in his room. To appease his parents, he has agreed to join a rowing club. He likes to go out with them to conferences and exhibitions. His parents are not worried about his future, but they are embarrassed because he does not fit into the legal framework of compulsory education. Under pressure from the school, they are caught between Eliott's choice, which they find logical, and the logic of a school which they understand cannot adapt to such a pronounced difference. They don't want to get their son in trouble, nor do they want to ruin their relationship by putting him under unnecessary stress. As there is no school in the region that offers an adapted education for children with very high potential, they see only one solution, a curriculum through the CNED, even if the school is not in favor of it. Eliott accepts the principle and specifies that he will do what is necessary to avoid causing problems for his parents.

Here again, the situation seems simple at first: a high potential, the gap with the other students, the boredom and the pleasure of living in his favorite universe. It is only when Eliott is seen alone that the complexity of his problem becomes apparent.

"I'm a smart ass, but I'm still afraid of others who criticize me. They think I'm a nerd, a mama's boy, a softie. All this makes me sad. You've been a student, so you know that school is a jungle and I don't want that.

I confirm him in his words. He continues:

- I don't see why I should have to endure this violent and stupid world, when I can travel as I want in my worlds where everything is beautiful. I go everywhere with my virtual helmet, and there I don't get bored. I go everywhere and I'm not afraid.

He adds that he documents himself in astronomy and that thanks to the virtual immersion, he travels in space-time.

- If you've seen the movie, it's kind of like *Interstellar*, an intergalactic journey, but in mine, it's still going well. I feel the contraction and expansion of space-time and when I come back I don't know where I am anymore. With that, I think I understood relativity and the fact that time is space, and space is time."

I confirm that I was interested in this film and that what it experiments with seems exciting. I add that he risks cutting himself off from the others a little more. He immediately shows me the opposite, arguing that it is thanks to this that he can bear our sad world. In our long discussions, he always has an answer for everything. Besides the pleasure of talking to him, I am fascinated by his timeliness. The parents admit that they can't stand his hypotheses and assertions, but they have confidence in their son who, they are sure, will be a brilliant researcher.

II - It's okay, I'll stop, I don't want any more!

Faced with his situation, I suggested to Eliott to put him in touch with an astrophysicist of my friends in order to find answers and to mark out his scientific thought, if it is one. Moreover, we decided with him and his parents to set up a home schooling program with the CNED while maintaining, thanks to the Apadhe[2] , a partial presence at school for two subjects, visual arts and life and earth sciences. It remains to approach the college to refine the individualized plan. The feedback given to the parents is a warning about the dangers of dropping out of school and the hypothesis of an autism spectrum disorder for Eliott. The main teacher asked for a check-up and, while waiting for a possible decision from Apadhe, insisted that their son go to school as often as possible. It is a real obsession of schools to want to put a label of ASD on differences, with the damaging confusion between high intellectual potential, which is not pathological, and an autism spectrum disorder. Moreover, this does not take into account the deleterious effect on Eliott, who does not want to be re-tested, nor does he want to be labeled "disabled".

Of course, the spectre of a prolonged withdrawal from school worries us because of the danger of desocialization, which is all the more risky as the difference becomes more pronounced over time outside the school environment. To avoid this, it is essential to establish, as conditions for a home curriculum, socialization initiatives in a preferred field and trials of new practices. For Eliott, these are exchanges with the astrophysicist, rowing, participation in an astronomy club and activities in a cultural center dedicated to digital worlds. All this has had a positive effect on his relationship with others, at least those who share his affinities and like to think.

At the same time, the psychotherapy allowed Eliott to soften the psychic defenses that had been put in place to protect him from the harassment he had suffered because of his difference, his high potential and his refusal to react to violence with violence. He recognizes

---

2.See details in the chapter "Schooling support systems".

that, under his attitude of *not even afraid, not even bad,* he had suffered from the humiliating remarks of the students, especially since he did not speak about it to anyone. His solution was to deny his injury while running away from the harassers, and therefore from the school. Remember that one out of every two cases of school phobia after the age of 6 is linked to school bullying. In Eliott's case, the rejection of school for reasons of boredom and loneliness concealed another reason, the traumatic anxiety linked to the harassment.

After a year of CNED home schooling, the parents decided to move to a town with an alternative school for children with high intellectual potential. Indeed, the partial integration in the school went rather badly: sickness of the art teacher, then several replacements to whom the parents had to explain the absences of their son. In addition, the teacher stigmatized Elliot during practical work in life and earth sciences, and some students refused to pair up with him, continuing to harass him despite the protective measures put in place. Finally, after a few weeks, Elliot did not attend this school at all, which, by the way, did not react or try to contact him, only reporting his absences and demanding proof that I provided in Eliott's interest. Today, he fits in remarkably well in his new alternative school where the educational project is really individualized.

Saying and doing: Meeting the Expectations of a High Potential Child

High intellectual potential is neither a disorder nor an illness, and even less the only reason for school failure and dropping out. It leads to a difference that must be taken into account in an individualized reception and teaching project. It is not because a school is not able to offer it or to protect from harassment that one should point out a so-called hypersensitivity which is only a reactivity to a disturbing environment, nor should one make it an autism spectrum disorder and designate the difference as an abnormality and handicap. Parents must ensure that their child is not pigeonholed or judged, nor is he or she the object of stigmatization and discrimination.

II - It's okay, I'll stop, I don't want any more!

One should not be afraid to implement a personal educational plan at home if measures are not taken to help the high potential child to find his place and to benefit from an education adapted to his abilities. Child psychiatrists are there to ensure that psychological suffering does not complicate the difference.

The parents of a high potential child have every interest in approaching associations to guide them in their search for an adapted establishment and original ways to make life more pleasant for the child and facilitate his socialization. These associations can also assist them in their efforts to integrate their child into the school system, particularly in terms of financing.

Today, there is a lot of talk about inclusion, about the right of every student to have a place in a mainstream school, regardless of his or her difficulties and differences. The reality is different: lack of resources and teacher training, overcrowded classes, lack of effort and concern on the part of the schools. From this damaging fact, and if the school establishment, which is understandable, does not have to do hand sewing, the National Education must recognize that it is unable to ensure a real inclusion of the child who is different or in difficulty. Let's make sure that we don't put the burden of this ineptitude on the child, that we don't mistreat him or his parents. If this is the case, do not hesitate to contact the Human Rights Defender.

I'm too comfortable in my room

I receive baffled parents who have requested a first appointment without their daughter, Jade, 15, who has not returned to school after the Covid lockdown. Out of school for five months and taking advantage of the chaotic in-person and distance learning situation, she managed to slip through the cracks for a year without getting to work. She has ignored teacher reminders. The parents don't know what to do, she flatly refuses to return to school. She told them so in a calm, determined manner, and when they insisted, she went into a violent crisis and threatened to run away. She told them that they didn't want to understand what she was doing since the lockdown, giving her much more than the high school, which offered her nothing and had no interest in her.

The situation is blocked because her parents are afraid she will do something stupid, run away or attempt suicide. At the same time, they notice that she is very active and creative in her room, which has practically become a recording studio. I am surprised, and her mother, embarrassed, replies:

"I have to admit that with telecommuting, all five of us were at home, along with his two brothers. The organization was very difficult and, in the end, everyone stayed in his room. We met for meals, if we can say "meet" because everyone was in front of his screen and left the table in a hurry to isolate himself again, including us. I am sorry, we only watched the children's work from a distance.

I reassure them, they did as they could, like many parents who were disoriented and distressed by the situation. It must be said that the beautiful stories during the confinement, if they exist, are not the majority. Loneliness, tensions, and even violence have been present in many homes disorganized by the confinement and anxiety related to the pandemic and the confinement.

The father adds:

- As soon as the confinement ended, her two brothers rushed to find their friends, their activities and the college, not for passion but just to see them again. On the other hand, Jade refused to go out, except to go shopping and on walks with us. If we don't talk to her about high school, I find her happy, full of energy and even much better than before the confinement. She has become more refined, she used to be a little wrapped up, she takes care of her appearance. She has become talkative, curious, she to whom we had to pull the wool over her eyes, shy and rather introverted. That reassures us, and that's why we want to avoid pushing her at all costs. In short, we come to see you when

II - It's okay, I'll stop, I don't want any more!

she's fine and not sick, it's just that she's refusing high school to devote herself to her activity."

Jade agrees to meet with me, although she finds it unnecessary. Such is the case with school refusals not justified by anxiety. She comes because she thinks I can fix things so that she will be left alone.

"I'm comfortable in my room and I don't want to go back to school, I have other things to do.

She explains to me that she has found her way and her job:

- Sure, I'm only 15 but now I know what I want and I'm able to do it on my own.

Then she describes to me her intense activity and what she has learned during these last months:

- Before the lockdown, I hated myself for being fat. I was ashamed, I hid under my *sweets*. When I was in my room, I was depressed, especially because it was violent, the social media *posts*, and I couldn't talk about it with my parents. They were always upset and stressed about telecommuting. I don't know how it happened, I found a way to react. I had been following an influencer for a while. I admired her, we talked together. She did me a lot of good. One day she challenged me, "You know, you're seriously beautiful, you could do what I do." At first, I didn't believe it, but in fact that's what saved me."

Jade started to take care of herself and to transform her look and style: diet that worried her mother but that she controlled, weight training, sheathing, hairstyle, make-up, clothing, all this under the benevolent look of the influencer, who became her friend. She discreetly placed orders for cosmetics, clothing and video equipment. She opened her YouTube channel and reactivated her social networks, mastering them thanks to her friend's advice. She read up on computers, business and law on the Internet. "In a few weeks, I learned a lot more than I did in a year in high school, thanks to my buddy who saved me from screwing up, getting hacked and running into a predator." Very invested in what has become a real job, Jade does not tire of this return on investment: she is loved, she is told she is beautiful, she even becomes an icon for some girls. Around a thousand *followers*, she is proud of this success in a short time, and does not intend to stop there. It is neither an addiction, nor a social phobic escape on the *hikikomori* mode, it is a real narcissistic construction thanks to the beneficial return on her image and her aptitudes in what she showed herself able to achieve.

Like her influencer friend, she runs her small business around her image and gives advice while learning about life and its ups and downs through her rich experience. She doesn't do business for the moment, but it's part of her plans when she manages to tell her parents about it. They hear her laughing and they begin to understand that she is not bored in her room, but they don't know what she really does there. She regrets that they are not interested, that they judge this job *as* superficial and that they only see danger in it. She does not perceive that her parents are seduced and even fascinated by the transformation of their daughter and what she is able to create. They have a legitimate fear like any parent who does not master social networks and knows the real risks.

I am also surprised to see the maturity and the quality of reflection of Jade, who is neither in the excess of management of her image (discreet make-up, sobriety of her presentation), nor in the drift of narcissistic omnipotence as the social networks push it. No sex, no product placement, no conspiracy, but valuable exchanges that teenage girls need, more than boys because they live a societal change where a rapid evolution in the status, place and affirmation of women takes place. If the risks of social networks are real (cyber harassment, incitement to radicalization, *fake news...*), if the addiction to digital and virtual poses a serious problem for the evolution of social relationships of teenagers and adults, a reasoned and intelligent use of these networks opens a new field of possibilities, and can even become a recourse to take care of oneself, as it is the case for Jade.

It is with this in mind that I must deal with Jade's de-schooling without upsetting her or compromising what she has built and which is very precious. As the school year progresses, we have agreed with

II - It's okay, I'll stop, I don't want any more!

her parents to postpone the reschooling until the following year and to allow her creative and rewarding endeavors to continue. I only ask that she reduce her screen time, especially the hours spent watching TV shows, and re-establish real life relationships with her former friends or even *followers*, which she prefers, in order to go on fresh ground instead. In short, she defended her choice well, like a businesswoman, which school does not prepare for at all, having a strong tendency to infantilize students, stressing them in the approach of continuous testing, the baccalaureate and Parcoursup, without opening them up to autonomy, self-management or the ability to elaborate a project from the draft to its realization. The only pedagogue and therapist was her influencer friend who put her in the saddle in a structuring and formative project. Thanks to her narcissistic gratifications, she helped Jade to build a rewarding image of herself and to let go of the desire to undertake without imitating her inspiration.

The following school year, Jade theoretically had to repeat her second year of school, she was 16 years old. If the school obligation is lifted at her age, an obligation of training intervenes, the interest of which is not to leave on the sidelines dropouts without diploma or training. For Jade, there is no question of going back to high school with girls she can't stand, that she finds immature and with whom she has lost contact, except for those who follow her on social networks. We understand her, but we will have to find a solution compatible with this obligation. Thanks to the local mission and an internship proposal with a future project in computer science or management, the solution is found.

The latest news, given by her parents, is that their daughter is progressing as an influencer and is starting to have contracts that bring her some income. In a way, Jade has become a *self-made-woman* with a significant educational background that allows her to surf on a wave as exciting as potentially profitable in one of these new professions. One can discuss the ethics of this but not the legitimacy, because it is in line with the evolution of society and is neither degrading nor alienating, provided that one is vigilant, which is the case for Jade, under the eye of her parents who are finally interested in what she is doing and support her business.

Saying and doing: should we accept that there is more to life than school?

Conventional schooling, whether general or technological, is not a panacea. If alternative schools are unfortunately rare, the alternatives proposed by some students deserve our full attention. *Self-made men and women* have always existed and have a double right to respect, that of a path they dare to take and that of a history that is often a journey of obstacles and trials of life.

The pandemic linked to the coronavirus has shaken up our certainties and our obviousness about work, school attendance, the meaning to be given to one's existence, the relationship to oneself, to one's image and to others. The filter of the digital and remote activity reshuffles the cards as much as the serious ecological crisis forces us to rethink our movements. Degrowth, at least the project to reduce anarchic growth and its effects on our world, which is running towards chaos and loss, is becoming more and more a just cause that young people have to defend. It is crucial to put the race for academic performance in this context and to listen to what some students no longer want, including those with the highest levels of education who refuse to subscribe to a system of excessive consumption and the destruction of the planet.

Pandemic and containment have produced the worst and the best in adolescents. From the passive withdrawal of *hikikomori* to the self-organization of Jade, from suicidal depression to creative fulfillment, it is the extinction or expansion of personalities that is at stake. A teenager on the fringe is not only synonymous with failure and danger, but on the condition that he is guided in his quest for himself, his true aspirations and the meaning he can and wants to give to his life.

Sacrosanct school, can we still learn differently and elsewhere? Certainly yes, what is not orthodox, standardized, can be valid, as evidenced by the alternative schools that start from the desire of

II - It's okay, I'll stop, I don't want any more!

students and trust their ability to feed their knowledge by themselves. The societal shift and the evolution of young people must encourage the National Education to review its concepts, not by adding more algorithms and controls. It is necessary to start from the aspirations and creativity of students and teachers, otherwise the de-schooling and the current dialogue of the deaf will only get worse. For Jade, the circumstances have been most favorable, but this is far from being the case for the majority who remain on the sidelines. We talk about dropouts without taking into account the fact that the National Education system has long since abandoned the objectives of education for all, of benevolence and respect towards the increasing number of students who cannot adapt to its rigid, abstract and imposed pedagogies, without any real plan to build the autonomy of future young adults.

Choosing, as Jade did, an alternative path to school obliges parents to set up clear markers so that their child does not go astray or get hurt, or even destroyed by contact with others. The risk is real, that of becoming an object caught up in narcissistic inflation that can put them at the mercy of predators. These markers also ensure that the experience gained is marked out with back and forth training. This must guarantee the possibility of bouncing back the day the alternative path is no longer suitable or does not work.

I don't give a fuck, I do what I want

He enters the office, jostling his mother as he goes. Who is this boy? I feel that this first interview will not be easy. I ask him what his name is and why he comes here. Hugo, 13 years old, answers, as I often hear, that he is not crazy, that he has nothing to do here, that he has already seen too many psychiatrists. And according to him, they only know how to prescribe medication and put him in a home, they don't understand anything and it will be the same with me. Faced with this aggressiveness and his rude words, his mother tries to moderate him. He stares at her with contempt, immediately cuts her off and makes a violent gesture. She is depressed, looks for support from me, powerless in front of this odious behavior. It is too early to intervene if it is not by a silent pause and a glance in direction of Hugo, what pushes him to call me. "You also think I'm crazy. You're going to shoot me up like the other shrinks and send me to the emergency room. That's nonsense, you are assholes. You too", addressing his mother before leaving the office abruptly. I continue the consultation with her mother. She says that she has tried everything, that she can't take it anymore, that he is very hard on his younger sister, that he is arrogant with everyone, including teachers, educators and anyone who gets in his way. He is constantly rebellious and opposed. Since he is rather intelligent, he always finds the right words, which leads to his rejection by several schools he has attended with the same result: exclusion for behavioral problems, insolence and violence. Each time, the mother was advised to have him treated, which she tried many times. Tests have identified a high intellectual potential. The only problem was that the neuropsychologist suggested an oppositional defiant disorder, because Hugo was constantly opposing and humiliating him. The neuropediatrician confirmed the hypothesis and prescribed Risperidone, a powerful antipsychotic that caused him to be considerably overweight and to feel chemically restrained, which, according to the mother, increased his rebellion to the point of hatred and systematic opposition to all educational measures. The placement in ITEP, a therapeutic, educational and pedagogical institute, allowed the mother to breathe a little and to take care of her daughter, sacrificed because of the mobilization around her son.

Hugo begged his mother to get him out of the ITEP and off medication, with many promises and seductive skills, which she accepted by setting her conditions of respecting the rules at home and at school. Was Hugo convinced that he would succeed by promising to follow them? In any case, as soon as school started, at the first remark of a teacher, he got carried away, left the class and went back home. Since then, he has refused to return to school for more than three months.

II - It's okay, I'll stop, I don't want any more!

He spends his time between playing video games in his room and hanging out with his friends in the neighborhood, with a few fights, but nothing serious. His mother can't say anything to him, she has chosen to appease him by giving up on educating him and making him apply the rules of good manners and participation at home. Under these conditions, he is rather helpful and sometimes takes care of his sister, even if he is always violent with her. He talks with his mother, who says she is exhausted by his intelligent argumentation but cannot stand any contradiction. She pretends to listen to him; when he realizes this, he gets angry. In spite of this, the atmosphere calms down until the de-schooling leads the social services to intervene following an information of concern for prolonged absenteeism without medical justification and racist remarks towards a foreign student. This is the reason why the mother asked me for a consultation, hoping to find a psychiatrist who would understand and help her son, and also help her in the face of the educational investigation decided by the judge. She would like to trust me but she doesn't believe in it too much, considering the previous experiences that have rather worsened the situation. Not that she blames these practitioners, but she is convinced that Hugo is unmanageable and will end up badly. Here is the challenge: why his revolt, his systematic opposition, his refusal of the authority, and how to untie it?

Faced with this threat from social services and the risk of a new placement, Hugo agreed to come and meet with me but with conditions: no medication or tests. When I ask him about his refusal to return to school, he is defensive:

"I don't give a shit, I do what I want.

To which I reply:

- Do you really know what you want?

- Anyway, not from being here, I hate psychiatrists, they all think I'm bad when I'm fine."

Hugo is an ultra-defensive bunker but ready to react aggressively to the slightest attempt to question his inner feelings, probably for fear of being destabilized, which seems unthinkable for him. So we talk about things: politics, science fiction, ecology... I notice that his intelligence is limited by his systematic defensive opposition posture which hinders his reflection. I tell him that it is really a pity to have a silly reasoning when one is intelligent like him. Interloqued, he lowers his voice and starts asking questions about my experience, my children and my passions. I answer him *minimally*, which allows him to feel respected by finding, he hopes, someone worthy of respect. Thanks to his explanations, I understand that it is a question of finding a father who can stand the road, solid, his being absent and failing. He left the family home when Hugo was 2 years old, without seeing him for several years. He reappeared when Hugo was 9 years old, already relevant and arrogant. Faced with this son who reproached him for his failure, the father never gave any sign of life, which resulted in a repetition of abandonment without hope or illusion, except for repeating his situation of rejection, secretly hoping that someone would one day be able to take up the challenge and not reject him. It was only after I had verified that I could hold this place that Hugo began to put down his arms and to be able to express his sensitivity, his inner pain, his sadness that had been well hidden behind his rebellious oppositional behavior. The treatments and the placements have, of course, only aggravated this experience of rejection, of abandonment that he also constantly re-enacts with his mother. He hopes that she will not let him go as the others have done, and for good reason, since he makes sure that he is rejected. He closes this diabolical circle on himself, and it is that which one must succeed in opening.

I hasten to complete the accompaniment by that of an educator practising in private practice, whose commitment, benevolence and firmness I know in order to help Hugo and his mother, and to neutralize by anticipating, if it is still possible, the intrusion of the social services which risk repeating, by the educational constraints, the maltreatment to which Hugo will push them. Then, I complete the securing and the protection of Hugo by setting up a course at home by the CNED.

II - It's okay, I'll stop, I don't want any more!

He accepted it without promising that he would follow it. All of these actions gradually bore fruit, provided a certain amount of patience and perseverance was shown in accompanying Hugo and his mother, not forgetting his sister who was severely tested by her brother's behavior. The setting up of a new educational framework with the restoration of the maternal authority was the business of the educator who, in a way, acted as a substitute father, including for the mother whose history was also marked by paternal mistreatment. This was repeated with Hugo's father, then with Hugo, himself replaying the abuse.

So I ask myself a question: why was this work of elaboration with Hugo not done during the previous treatments with psychologists and psychiatrists? This is a naïve question, because one must be motivated and have the desire to commit oneself in order to succeed in a true encounter, in the sense of discovery, curiosity and benevolence without *preconceived ideas*, in order to understand this repetitive behavior of failure, provocation and rejection on the part of a child who, at first sight, is detestable. In fact, he hides his suffering behind his arrogance which is all the more unbearable because he puts all his intelligence into it. Faced with this, the evaluation and diagnosis systems deliver their response in the form of repressive stigmatization. They are based on categories into which the child is fitted, without taking into account the substance of the problem. Then, there is nothing left to do but to apply re-education measures, placement, and to treat the disturbing symptoms with psychotropic drugs that are supposed to be effective. This is what Hugo has been going through for several years, and this downward spiral must be stopped. How can we make professionals understand that by doing this they are only aggravating the problems? One cannot blame the school administration or the teachers who are not trained, have neither the time nor the availability for this meeting, except for some remarkable exceptions. On the other hand, the care-givers are *a priori* trained to treat with humanity and according to the latest scientific data. However, professionals in neuropsychological care have seized upon formatted classifications rather than seeking this quality of encounter with a child or adolescent in pain. Their algorithm does not aim to understand the young person by focusing on recent scientific data and even less by respecting a holistic dimension[3] taking into account all the data of the child's problem. The algorithm is limited to one axis: disorder, therefore assessment, therefore handicap, therefore rehabilitation and medication. For Hugo, the result was catastrophic, and the challenge to stop the infernal spiral of rejection was enormous. He was not treated but evaluated, judged, placed in an institution and under chemical restraint. This only aggravated his aggressive revolt. Hugo is like a dog in a cage who is enraged, so he is put down, and, frightened, in danger, in a state of desperation, he is ready to bite anyone who comes near.

Intelligent, Hugo follows easily and by far his curriculum at the CNED. He chose, under the guidance of his educator, to turn to urbex, between jumps and climbing in the city. His overweight and his lack of muscular strength encouraged him to follow a physical rehabilitation program in which he invested himself remarkably, transforming his clumsy body into a teenager's body athletic enough to perform in urbex. All the people involved, including his mother, have been instructed never to approach him head-on, but to appeal to his intelligence and reflection so as not to awaken in him this wild beast ready to bite and not to repeat the spiral of rejection. He is not ready to go back to school, but it doesn't matter as long as he follows the CNED curriculum and thrives in socializing activities. Between Hugo and the caring people who accompany him, a moral contract has been made: respect for the word given and the promises made, mutual respect, asking for help without aggression, not hurting anyone, practicing empathy, following to the letter the rules elaborated with the educator and his mother, thinking about the consequences of his actions before acting. This framework

---

3. The holistic approach of the human being takes into account all the elements that make up his or her existence: biological, neuropsychological, socio-familial and environmental.

has allowed the restoration of a peaceful family life. Of course, there are still slips when he is upset or feels like a failure.

Hugo also decided to meet his father, in the hope of having a man who would stand up to him. He took this risk, not without anxiety, thanks to the solid presence of the educator and my psychotherapeutic support. The meeting was not what he had hoped for, having found himself facing a man who was fallen, inconsistent and addicted to alcohol.

Saying and doing: dealing with defiant and violent school refusal

When faced with a teenager's difficult behaviour and his or her withdrawal from school due to exclusion or escape from the constraints of the school environment, the real reason for this disturbing behaviour must not be overlooked.

If a diagnosis and treatment are necessary when the behavioral problems are serious and push the child or adolescent into a downward spiral, it is only after having done everything possible to meet him, understand him, and help him through psychotherapy conducted without *preconceived ideas*, judgments, or rejections.

The information of concern sent to the president of the departmental council (CRIP) is all the more unwelcome as it appears to the young person and his family as a threat of acquisition and placement. This worrying information has become a means of pressure from education and care professionals, which is used more and more. It is all the more worrying when it stigmatizes the child who has been taken out of school for a behavioral disorder, whether the taking out of school is due to an exclusion or to the child running away. If the worrying information can inaugurate a medical-social help when nothing has been done until then and when the family and school situation becomes very critical, we notice that very often it worsens the difficulty of the parents who feel judged and betrayed rather than helped. This is all the more destructive since they have often already done their best to help their child.

Yes, the intervention of the social services following this worrying information can be a precious help, provided that they are dealing with professionals who are concerned about helping, supporting and accompanying the child and his parents without moral judgement or untimely intervention (consultation or imposed assessment, intrusion in medical secrecy, placement...).

There is always a possible approach that responds to a behavioral problem, even if it is serious. It remains to find the right angle of action, the right professionals to be accompanied and eventually treated. The goal is not schooling at all costs and as quickly as possible, it is to resolve what is hidden by the behavioral problem, which often has a psychic, psychosocial, and sometimes also neuronal origin.

It's too hard, they give us too much work

A tall girl arrives in my office, her long hair hiding her face, surrounded by her parents. A funeral procession, I expect a dramatic announcement. During the first interview and the following ones, I will not see Clémence's face and will have to listen to hear the few words she utters in her dull voice. The parents explain the situation. Their daughter has joined the lycée in seconde, European section. She is an excellent student, studious but a perfectionist. She spends her evenings and weekends copying her lessons, learning them by heart, constantly checking and filing her cards so as not to forget anything. She chose the European section but found herself without friends. Her parents encouraged her, thought she was doing too much and asked her to rest. She refused to listen and stopped all distractive activities. What had to happen happened, as soon as the October vacations came around, she broke down and lay on her bed all day with her lessons next to her. But she was unable to concentrate, exhausted, mute, without appetite. In spite of everything, she tried to work because she did not want to give up.

The doctor prescribed a normal biological check-up and vitamins. To prove to her parents that she was better after the vacation break, she went back to school and worked hard despite the recommendations of her parents and the doctor. Two weeks before the Christmas vacations, when the exams were due, she refused to get up, told her parents that she was quitting school, locked herself in her room, and piled up her lessons in her closet. She emptied her surroundings, refused to talk to her parents or her friend, who was worried about her and tried to find a solution so that she wouldn't give up. The school suggested that she leave the European section, which required a lot of work. Her mother wanted her to rest first and foremost, while her father had an unfortunate comment to make: "*It's true, you should stop, maybe you're not cut out for this section,*" which triggered a violent crisis. She screams at him that there's no way she's going to stop, that she's capable but that the teachers are giving too much work and she can't take it anymore. She scratches her arms and face violently, screaming that she sucks, that she'll never make it, and that they all know it, starting with her brother and sister who despise their little sister and succeed at everything without making an effort, adulated by their father. She adds that she is the retard of the family, that her mother has never loved her and has always pushed her and at the same time devalued her. The parents were shocked and could not reassure her because they were so shocked by her words. They had no idea how much their daughter was suffering. How much pain, how many feelings of injustice and worthlessness she kept inside her without anyone noticing! At first, the parents blamed it on her exhaustion and a feeling of failure. Since then, they have been feeling guilty and overly attentive to their daughter who has become apathetic, mute and anorexic, as much as depressed.

It is in this context that I receive her with elements of understanding as to the seriousness of her condition, her loneliness and her suffering which, obviously, are not new. The Christmas celebrations, which she had enjoyed so much up to now, seem to have been an ordeal. She ate very little, did not open her presents. Yet, they were everything she had dreamed of before.

How their daughter could have formed these convictions of contempt and rejection on their part was incomprehensible. During a few meetings with her and her parents, we discussed the history and functioning of the family, without any event standing out and explaining Clémence's distress. Her condition obliges me to combine psychotherapy with a prescription for medication. which she accepts because she is extremely fearful of the hospitalization she is considering with her parents. If her words are partly linked to her deep malaise, they will be a thread of Ariadne's care. The parents understood that a return to school was not possible for a long time. It was difficult to make them understand that, like the employee who was suffering at work, their daughter was experiencing a burn-out, complicated by a masked depression that was revealed during the school burn-out. Clémence collapses when she realizes that her year of second grade is compromised but, deep down, she is relieved. I see her every week and prescribe her an antidepressant and anxiolytic treatment.

Little by little, the vise loosens. While continuing to hide in her hair, she starts, by dint of warm solicitations from me, to express her deep feeling of being useless and useless, of having a *shitty life*, of being ugly and stupid. It is not from her antics or the expectation of recognition, she is convinced of it. Her condition struggles to improve but she eats a little more and manages to sleep. In a monotone, without palpable emotion, as if disembodied and indifferent to the signs of affection of those around her, she says that she is a little better, rather to reassure those around her than out of conviction. She refuses to go down to the living room when her brother and sister, in higher education, come home. She doesn't want to see her friend who still dares to knock on her door. It was several weeks before she agreed to come out of her room and help her parents with their business. She does it without enthusiasm, whereas, until now, she had made it her mission to take over, interested in the business and thinking that her father would be satisfied, he who regretted that his eldest son did not want to take over the business. *I understood that for him, I was an alternative. It's true,*

II - It's okay, I'll stop, I don't want any more!

I liked this job, but now it's over," says Clémence, who no longer feels anything and questions everything, to the point of not finding any meaning in her past and present life. As for the future, there is no more, depression obliges. She is convinced that she has failed to be loved by both her mother and her father. So she does what she has to do like a robot, just to give the change. *It's too late, I have disappointed them all. I don't belong here anymore.* The suicidal thoughts are increasing, or rather finally expressing themselves in place of the silence. The treatment doesn't seem to be working, and yet she is changing a little.

If the therapy seems to be well underway, to allow her to move forward, one or more elements are missing, whose emotional and depressive sideration indicates the traumatic character. Clémence manages to express, first of all, what she had suffered at elementary school, again harassment linked to the fact that her father is a notable person in the small town and that she is doing well at school. Depreciation, humiliation, inappropriate gestures, she did not speak about it to her parents, keeping it deep inside her, ashamed and convinced of being ugly and too much on earth. I ask her a deliberately naive question: *Why didn't you talk about it?* She finally starts to cry, saying that her parents wouldn't have believed her, that they thought the same thing about her anyway. After a long silence, she says that all this is nothing compared to what her sister did to her. She explains that, as a child, she was already under her yoke, that she was subjected to her touching without understanding anything and under the threat that *if you say it, I will say all the stupid things you do.* That fixed the obligation for Clémence to never say anything whereas her stupidities were tiny, even non-existent compared to the incestuous acts of her big sister.

Thanks to her very painful revelation, I am beginning to understand, and she is beginning to understand, what was behind this *burn-out that* looked like a reactionary depression: a severe, traumatic infantile depression, which had been masked until then by her defensive construction as a student aiming to be perfect. To achieve this, she forced herself to work a lot because the cognitive barriers linked to the trauma and the psychic stupefaction obliged her to make an incessant effort to fight against her feelings of guilt and depreciation.

The experience of abandonment on the part of her parents has as much to do with the obligation to keep quiet and to conceal her supposed guilt and shame as with the admiration they have for this sister who is doing brilliant studies. The worst thing is that Clémence, convinced that she is no match for her, also admires her sister. She has nothing to do on this earth, which allows us to understand the strength of her suicidal ideas, but not yet to stop them. Seeing herself submerged and failing, or so she thought, in her challenge of a second year in the European section, whereas her sister had followed an Abibac section, and she was perfectly bilingual, this signs her impossibility of repairing herself through revenge, and therefore her death warrant. We can see that over the years silence has done its work. It eroded her narcissistic construction, aggravated her contempt for herself in the identification with the aggressor, her sister and, later, the harassing students who violated her intimacy.

How to get out of this impasse? Neither medication nor the acknowledgement of what she has suffered can help her. It is impossible to extract the stone of melancholic madness linked to the trauma and the abandonment. On the other hand, after having let the black bile of her depression and her infantile suffering flow out, I had to help her start a fight for herself. No matter how much her parents and her brother and sister disliked her, she had to get out of the silence, she had to talk about her traumas, she had to express her suffering, she had to make her feelings of abandonment, of failure and of being unloved understood. One must succeed in being heard. Instead, Clémence postponed her appointments, fleeing from them, and reinforced her isolation while giving the impression that she was the family business.

This is often where psychotherapy stumbles, in the face of the dread that is the struggle to exist. It takes unconditional support and effective mediation by the therapist to achieve this without rushing but with determination. Talking with her mother, hearing her parents'

II - It's okay, I'll stop, I don't want any more!

condemnation of her sister, waiting for her apology or considering a trial that could be even more devastating, this is what she fears most. This is what we managed to do, for the time being without a trial, and which allowed Clémence to resume her studies. Finally, she left the European section to join a section that directs her towards the profession she has chosen, that of her father, but in a spirit other than to be loved by her parents and to wait for her father's recognition. It is a question for her to occupy her place without being the little sister, the little failure, but in a certain way the heiress. It is a healthy revenge, an accomplishment and the beginning of a narcissistic consistency which enables her to compare herself less with her brother and her sister and which reduces, but it is not gained, her strong tendency to devalue herself.

Who could have imagined that behind *it's too hard, they give us too much work was* hidden such an infantile trauma, organizer of a future programmed chaos? Elements indicated that it was not a question of looking for an immediate solution, between rest and change of section, which is sometimes enough but not in his case. It was necessary to decide the parents, especially the father, to accept to live a blank year for a dark period, the only way to get out of the melancholy and the traumatic stupefaction. It was necessary to take the time to understand and to draw the Ariadne's thread. In my opinion, this is the only way to avoid compromising Clémence's chances of a life that will not be made up only of depression, or even suicide.

Saying and doing: what to do when a childhood trauma resurfaces?

Adolescence is too important a period in the psychic reorganization to be satisfied with small measures and blind tinkering in order to put the young person back on his feet.

If we accept that an adult suffering from *burn-out* or exhaustion depression should be off work for a period of about six months, why do we have so much trouble accepting it for a child or adolescent who is suffering or exhausted? It is true that it is difficult to accept that one's child is sick, because he or she is young, because he or she has a life ahead of him or her, because he or she has nothing to complain about, because he or she has everything to be happy. But it's not that simple: treating his suffering is both an emergency and a prevention. Although school is very important, in dramatic situations such as that experienced by Clemence, it is not a priority. The prolonged absence from school is a medically justified sick leave. This avoids the impasse of running away and failing at school.

In a society where performance and time management are imposed from school onwards, it is not surprising that things sometimes break down. Too much work in certain sections, docile and studious children who do not want to disappoint parents and teachers, but also children who are unavailable at times depending on their preoccupations, their anxiety and the events they have experienced or are currently experiencing. To help them, we must let them rest, ask themselves the right questions. Sometimes it's not the time, something more important needs to be dealt with before they are available for school.

Medication use for children and adolescents is a delicate matter. It should never be the first step. None of the medications used by psychiatrists will cure the root of any problem, but they do have their uses. Therefore, prescribing them is not dangerous, but on the condition that they are correctly chosen and used *at* an adjusted dose. For the child, as for the adult, anxiety and depression can produce unbearable suffering which, in itself, will be traumatic and insurmountable without a medicinal contribution.

I don't need school to do what I want to do

The current trend is to bring a child or adolescent who has dropped out of school and school learning to psychologists and child psychiatrists. It is a step forward to question possible psychological difficulties at the origin of this dropout symptom. But it also runs the risk of psychologizing the situation, which is a different matter: social, educational, institutional and political. For example, a young girl, 16 years old, agreed, not without difficulty, to her parents' request to consult a psychiatrist because she had deliberately stopped going to school. She says to me, very determined: *I don't need to go to school anymore to do what I want to do.* I ask the parents what I have to do with this because there seems to be no malaise or anxiety. It is a choice affirmed by their daughter. However, the situations outlined in the previous chapters show that an argumentative statement and seemingly clear thinking can conceal a complex situation. In other words, when a young person comes for help, it is better not to trivialize the situation and to take the time to analyze the ins and outs of the school refusal.

Elsa was directed towards a BEP in hotel and restaurant management, a choice by default, given her low grades and her lack of affinity with school. As soon as she started her first internship, she was dismissed because she did not respect the rules, got into trouble with the customers and with the head waiter. As a result, she did not go to school for two months. I receive her alone because she refuses to speak with her parents. She explains that they don't want to understand anything, that she has other aspirations in life than to undergo and submit to *asshole customers,* to be a slave to a boss who thinks he is her father and who, on top of that, has humiliated her in front of the waiters. Moreover, she doesn't want to work for a miserable salary and have lousy hours that cut her off from her friends. Obviously, she is not made for this kind of job, if one can be, the post-covid disaffection for these difficult jobs of the restoration testifies it. In short, it is out of the question that she continues in this branch. She adds that offering her another one is *not even a dream.* I asked her what she was thinking about, and then her face radiated, she could not stop talking about her projects, which I sensed from her appearance: a beautiful young woman with a lot of make-up, a somewhat outrageous style, very sparse in fabric, which let her advantageous shapes show.

Elsa tells me about her steps: registration to the Miss contest of her department, multiple contacts for castings of extras, reality shows, presence on TV sets, in short, even if she knows that at 16 years old many doors are closed to her, she shows herself efficient in her steps oriented towards the *star system* where her body is a great asset. Her dream is to be selected for a reality show, where one earns a lot of money and has a chance to become a star, her ultimate goal. Immediately, she explains to me that she will not do anything, that, contrary to what her parents say, she *will not fall into the gutter* and that she is tired of being called a *whore. Just because I'm beautiful and have an attractive body doesn't mean I'll give myself to anyone. I just have to find my agent and, with that, I will earn a lot of money.* To achieve this, she multiplies *selfies* and contacts production agencies known for their reality shows around the world.

After having listened to her, I receive her parents and tell them to watch over her while taking into account her approach which, in itself, seems to be an education, provided that it is conducted with caution. We leave it at that after having heard the parents' recriminations and fears about this depraved environment where their daughter risks getting lost. While understanding their anxiety, I answer: *It depends on your vigilance and your accompaniment with her, which must remain positive. Your daughter is projecting herself into the zeitgeist even if it is not the future you dreamed of for her.* They are confused and insist that she is unmanageable, that she goes out whenever she wants and that she spends her life on social networks where she keeps posting her *selfies*. She is proud that everyone looks at her in the street because she is so provocative. Even if I understand the arguments and the fear of her parents, there is not much to do for them, except listen to them.

I received them a month later, with the intention of guiding them in the accompaniment of their daughter so that she would not go astray, that she would not fall into the hands of predators who are numerous around very young and beautiful girls like her. In the meantime, they have resumed the dialogue with Elsa by trying to understand her and

II - It's okay, I'll stop, I don't want any more!

to be positive but also to follow her steps. They accompany her for her castings in Paris, which makes her feel safe and allows them to support her when she is refused, which is the frequent conclusion of the interviews.

A few weeks later, I received a call from Elsa who begged me to see her as soon as possible, which I did of course. She had just lived a detestable experience. It was to be expected, she had been deceived and mistreated by a recruiter who had taken advantage of her naivety, whatever she might say, in the face of the skillful manipulation capacity of this kind of predator who flatters and promises, in order to better take advantage of these young girls who hope so much to be part of the rare chosen ones during reality TV castings. *I thought I was strong enough to resist, but this bastard fooled me. I won't be fooled again and I'm going to do everything I can.* After describing the situation, from which she finally came out quite well without any real trauma, we look at what she could do, with the idea of getting her into training so that she is better equipped for life. What the French education system offers does not suit her, too far from reality, too infantilizing, with no prospects. Elsa decided to take a course in English, or rather in American, because she had not lost sight of her goal of living in Los Angeles or Miami, among the stars, even though she was aware that this could be a lure and a source of painful disillusionment. I propose to complete it with a training in audiovisual and management which will be a plus in the project she aspires to. She approaches the local mission, the contact goes badly, she feels judged and they want her to return to the BEP. On her own, with the support of her parents, she found a training program adapted to her expectations in Belgium, far from the French school system. Three months later, she sent an e-mail: *"An informed woman is worth two, enough to defend herself against predators. I am armed, thank you. If you have a moment, you can see me in a TV show about young people, I send you the link. I also signed a contract as an extra in Brussels, that's great.* Of course, I watch her, and see her very comfortable in this show where she tells her teenage

I Don't Want to Go to School Anymore

journey. I'm surprised by her timeliness and logic when she talks about dropping out. About school: *They take us for kids, they infantilize us with all these tests and grades. If we're not nice, we're put in detention like a little kid in a corner.* About the teachers: There is a *lot of injustice and that doesn't make you want to work. You wonder who they think they are, they're scornful, distant, you feel like you're pissing them off. What disgusted me the most was that they humiliated you in front of the whole class. Fortunately, they're not all like that. And if I hadn't had a great PE teacher, I would never have dared to do what I do. He gave me back my confidence. He told me that I was capable of succeeding and that I would make my own way. That's exactly what's going on. But I was so disgusted that I didn't do anything in class. That's why they put me in a BEP without giving me a choice. I ended up in the hotel and restaurant business, which really sucked.* Then, with her voice freed, she continues about her life: *We should be better prepared for life, to know how to manage ourselves and to deal with problems in real life. Instead of spending our time learning math and grammar, even though it's important for those who like it, we should be told how to have a good job and choose according to who we are.* It is true that she seems better prepared for life than most teenagers, kept away from the problems they will have to solve in their relational and socio-professional life. To acquire knowledge is one thing, certainly useful, but to know how to use it and to overcome the obstacles in order to realize oneself is another thing that also requires learning.

One year later, new email: *I signed up for an acting class, which is great, and I understood that there was more to life than my body. At least now I'm not at the mercy of guys who just want to jump on me. Thank you for helping me.* This rather happy conclusion shows that her parents did the right thing in seeking the help of a child psychiatrist, even though she didn't seem to need one at all. She went from a delusion centered on her beautiful body, which gave her some advantages, to the realization that it was a trap for a woman to be the object of men, their greed and their schemes. English, audiovisual, management and

11 - It's okay, I'll stop, I don't want any more!

theater, finally, she manages her early career remarkably well and she can trust both her assets and her insight and intelligence of life.

To say and to act: to study and to accept the choice of a new way

Let's not lose sight of the fact that there may be real and, in the end, quite legitimate reasons for the student to drop out of school by means of a well-considered decision, without anxiety. It would be a double punishment for the student to be blamed for an injustice, a forced orientation, an abuse of the school environment that discriminates or stigmatizes.

Meeting with a psychiatrist, even if there are no worrying psychological signs, can be useful, if only to talk between parents and children and to raise the issue of dropping out. As Elsa's case shows, even if the help of a child psychiatrist did not seem necessary at *first*, it proved useful by proposing an accompaniment of her choice that was both new and delicate.

To be satisfied with the school's contribution in order to hope to form a child is to fail. It is to give the school a mission that it is incapable of assuming, an objective that it cannot achieve. The accompaniment of parents, life experiences and relationships, all this is at least as precious as the knowledge acquired in school.

Why limit what some educational teams do for dropouts to a few experiments, without supporting them or making them permanent, or extending the application to all those who request it? The quality of training and academic achievement would only be improved.

Proximity, attention and project should remain the strong axes of all teaching so that knowledge is always associated with experience and that every student is solicited from his best angle, where he is the most receptive and creative.

A pedagogy that would give itself the means of a case-by-case approach would certainly be more costly at the outset but more profitable in its long-term results. It is not certain that governments, even in a democracy, seek to train autonomous people with a good critical capacity. It is more convenient to aim to train good employees, adaptable and flexible workers, and even, if necessary, cannon fodder. The result is disinterest and disinvestment that translates into professional, civil and civic life.

An original and atypical training path is no more dangerous than a well-trodden path that requires a diploma. When desire and creativity are present, it is a guarantee of success. It remains to mark out and supervise this original path in order to avoid dead ends and failures because, by definition, adolescents are easy prey for predators and perverts.

You know I suck. You said it yourself!

I receive a mother in consultation who drags her son, apathetic and slumped. She comes because she is worried about a decision that the school is urging her to make in view of the poor results of Bryan, 14 years old, in 4th grade after having repeated 5th grade. He was not yet mature enough to face middle school. Despite everyone's efforts to help and stimulate him in his school work, Bryan did not seem to invest himself or make an effort. The picture is bleak, which he acknowledges while mumbling that he is trying but not succeeding. He should be entering a 3rd year pre-professional program[4] . His mother fears that this is a mistake that will lead to failure because he is neither practical nor skilled with his hands, except for using his console controller. Bryan adds:

"They don't get it, if you put me there, I'll do even less. Remember, they already wanted me to go to the SEGPA with the dumb ones. That means it's dead. Anyway, the other guy is right. He says I suck and I won't get anywhere.

---

4. Now called "3e prépa-métiers", this orientation is designed to inform students about different professions.

What other person is he talking about without naming him? His mother states:

- With his father, it's a bit of a war. He doesn't want to see him anymore because, every time he goes there, his father devalues him by telling him that he is good for nothing, that he doesn't do anything, that he will become unemployed and that he will end up on the street with the bums.

Bryan interjects, very emotional:

- Please, Mom, stop. Don't tell him, if he finds out I'm going to prep school, I'm dead, I'm good for a beating."

He goes from an apparent casualness to a sadness and fear that surprises his mother. Indeed, with her as with the others, he never shows anything. He is as if he is indifferent to what surrounds him and, as a result, he receives the same kind of reflection from his teachers and his mother, who is fed up with his inertia and his failure.

In spite of everything, she understands him and specifies that his father is hard with him and does not let anything pass. She doesn't push him to go and see this father who has founded his new family and doesn't really care about his son, except to *yell at him* and she adds:

"Bryan has been through a lot, his father was abusive to me, and since the divorce, he denigrates me to him. Now he has a little girl and he takes care of her a lot. Bryan denies it, but he must be jealous. It's normal, he didn't get all that."

Quiet. It's time to talk to Bryan alone.

The question of the orientation in pre-professional school becomes the salutary pretext to evoke the painful situation of Bryan who deploys efforts of passive inertia and indifference to show nothing of his suffering. All his psychic energy is mobilized not to crack nor to show himself weak. But he also needs to prove this father right, to prove to himself that he is useless. In fact, he sinks into a behaviour of failure which comes from his depression and the duel opposition/appeal of this father who only knows how to devalue him. Without being aware of it, he provokes the negative attention of this man and, at the same time, he especially does not want to satisfy this one whom he names "the other", to whom he denies a place of father that he does not deserve.

Bryan's mask has just cracked by hearing his mother. This is the prerequisite for him to get out of his impasse, to identify the trap in which the paternal abandonment places him, increased by the denigration of both his mother and himself. How much suffering does he live in solitude, how much energy does he deploy to show nothing of his weakness! And how much time is wasted and future compromised because of such mistreatment, how much morbid repetition to prove to himself that he sucks, and that his father is really right! Bryan has turned the gun on himself. He has the same behavior of morbid repetition with the teachers, from whom he hears the sad music of his nullity, his laziness, his sad future destiny. By his orientation in pre-professional school, he achieves a destructive goal, the signature of his failure to be loved, to be recognized, to value himself and to try to build a narcissism by valuing himself otherwise than by his casual style. Paradox of the situation, he always has in him the hope that this father recognizes him as a good son but he knows that it will not happen, then he anticipates the disappointment which would not fail to arrive in case he would make all his efforts to satisfy him:

"In fourth grade, I realized that it was no longer going to help. Every time, he only saw what was wrong. He didn't care about me, broke me whenever I made a mistake at school and even for everything I did. My mother told you that I was not good with my hands. I know why: every time I built something, I liked it, he said I couldn't do anything with my ten fingers, and that it sucked, so I stopped. It's true, I admit I don't try too hard. Now the only thing I care about is my console. I'm not bothered about that.

Above all, don't show anything, don't lose face, but above all, don't think because this would expose Bryan, like other children who live an unspeakable inner suffering, to the reactivation of a deep feeling of abandonment. The mother, who does everything for her son, cannot fill the void left by the father's absence. Especially since, wanting to

II - It's okay, I'll stop, I don't want any more!

compensate for the father's insufficiencies, she has softened his education to the point of leaving Bryan facing a vacuum of authority which, rather than filling the abandonment, digs it a little more. Worse, in an attempt to smooth things over, she tried to excuse the father's behavior, which Bryan interpreted as validation of his worthlessness.

Not to think is to be absent, suspended in one's *no-man's land* without listening to anything the teachers say. Why is this? Again, to avoid setting himself up for failure, convinced that he will not understand anything, and to avoid the risk of hearing the negative and humiliating comments of teachers who despair of such an attitude. Attention deficit, concentration deficit, comprehension deficit, and above all, a thought deficit that flees from learning in order not to confront his own narcissistic flaw. Deep down, Bryan is caught up in a persecutory process in anticipation of the negative judgement made of him. The loop closes because he does everything to make this judgment fall and condemn him to nullity. Unless one is particularly perceptive, it is logical that everyone, including the teachers, will fall for it.

In Bryan's case, we shouldn't expect a miracle, just because he understood the trap we put him in and he put himself in. I'm going to help him on two levels. On the one hand, I will challenge his legendary clumsiness, his lack of practicality, his alleged inability to consider his professional training in technical fields and so-called manual trades. On the other hand, I defend in his eyes the 3rd year of pre-professional training, which is neither a dead end nor a signature of failure, but an opportunity to prove his intelligence and his ability to learn, experiment and discover different trades until he hopes to click and commit himself. He accepts the omen because he finds with me, his shrink, as is often the case in these cases, an opener, not to say a benevolent father figure. It is possible that this opener is one of his teachers or an educator, a facilitator, a training master, but so far, it has not happened. Such an encounter is capable of stopping the process of morbid repetition and, at the same time, of initiating or consolidating the construction of a positive self-image capable of success. This is the case for Bryan, who has recently embarked on a vocational course of study in which he is doing well, and accepts a virtuous circle of recognition of his abilities.

Bryan didn't miss any appointments, except for one. We had agreed (in fact, I had pushed him) to a meeting with his father to try to make him understand that his son was neither incapable nor lazy, but suffered from the lack of a benevolent look from him. On the day of the appointment, no Bryan, he had, deliberately or not, left me alone with his father. He was probably expecting a lot, but he was under no illusion that he would hear negative things that would undermine the effort he had been making since the beginning of his psychotherapy. In fact, he was right, the father stuck to his guns, while denigrating psychology. He turned the tables, blaming his mother's poor upbringing on his every whim and making him into nothing more than a flabby rag. Obviously, the grievances towards his ex-wife prevented him from looking at Bryan as his son and from holding his place as a father. The pampered child of a hated mother, the son of an immature man, that was the place, or rather the lack of place, that he gave to his son. At the next appointment, Bryan waited, moved, for my comment without wanting to show his impatience. I told him that he had to deal with his father's failure, that he had to rely on the beautiful encounters he was making in his professional training and with his friends. It is difficult, much more than we think, to mourn what we did not have. There is nothing left to hold on to, neither memories nor kindness, you just have to deal with it. To draw a line on a father, a mother, that is sometimes necessary to build oneself without destroying oneself, but it is not easy to live. Very often, it is a scar that never closes.

Say and do: how to fight against passive absenteeism?

There are so many ways to flee school, from dropping out of school through truancy expansion to refusal through opposition, through anxiety, but we forget the most common, frequent, probably the most terrible, passive absenteeism: I am there without being there, I am absent from myself and from learning. Basically, I don't exist, that's the misunderstanding. This child is judged to be lazy, poor in spirit. We believe him, and he believes himself to be useless, whereas very often, his presence/absence only translates a suffering.

When a parent denigrates his child directly or through his teachers and school, he deprives him of being the student receptive to knowledge and discovery. A fog, even a wall, is erected between the degraded child and the student he should be if he were encouraged. Worse, if the teacher gets involved and adds thickness to this wall, it becomes impassable. It takes tremendous strength to help the teacher break down that wall and restore the child's confidence.

Technological and vocational courses of study deserve respect and esteem. Indeed, the teaching and experience they provide is as valuable as that of the so-called general courses of study, which are considered prestigious because they deal with abstract subjects. An effort has been made to improve the image of the professional, but the fact remains that these subjects are still considered by parents and teachers to be of zero level. How then can we expect a student to see himself as anything other than a waste product?

To learn, one must not only be receptive, but also capable of thinking. If the act of thinking comes across a painful feeling of failure, the thought becomes evil, and one must flee from it. The best way to do this is for some students to flee and despise thought, to see it only as a flaw in order to avoid their own. Apparent stupidity is often only the escape from oneself.

Teachers, some of whom are excellent at it, and parents deploy a great deal of ingenuity to make their child, walled up in his incapacity, want to take the risk of proving to himself that he is, contrary to what he has been made to believe and to what he has come to think, capable of succeeding. The most difficult thing is to help them break down the wall of indifference, stupidity and self-denigration.

III - SHOULD WE TRUST THE SOLUTIONS FOUND BY THE CHILD?

While schools, health care professionals and parents seek and find (not always, unfortunately) solutions between adaptation, accommodation and care, it is not uncommon for children, especially adolescents, to propose their own solutions based on their feelings, their needs, their experience and that of their friends. It is useful to look at them even when they seem quite strange and unheard of. Before following any solution, it is important to explore its feasibility, pitfalls and consequences in the short, medium and long term.

In order to solve a problem, it is necessary to have understood the statement, which we have done throughout the chapters by evoking the complexity and diversity of situations of refusal and academic blocking. In each case, we need to outline the ways in which they can be tackled and resolved. It remains to complete the panel of possible solutions for parents, teachers, care and education professionals when faced with a school refusal that resists common sense, school directives and care adjusted as closely as possible to the child's problem.

Children and teenagers are not left out to find a solution that suits them. They talk among themselves, sometimes passing on tricks like cheat sheets that slip from hand to hand. The risk is that they see above all their immediate interest, their pleasure and sometimes the avoidance of the effort that school learning and the rules of life in the community require, *a fortiori* in a school based on discipline. Sometimes professionals, even those with long experience, are fooled by a well-orchestrated presentation of anxiety, alleged harassment by a stalker or exhaustion that is not linked to exhausting school work but to the hours spent at night in front of the screens. It is sometimes difficult to find your way around, especially since you should not miss out on real exhaustion, anxiety or harassment. It is better to anticipate the worsening of the situation and the danger of suicide, at the risk of finding oneself (this happens more often than one would think) confronted with a young person who, once his or her withdrawal at home has been validated, settles down in a *cocooning environment* and no longer comes to consult a doctor, since he or she is comfortable there and has finally obtained exactly what he or she wanted.

In fact, the real good solution is usually found together (child, parents and professionals) by taking the time to dialogue and to clearly state the problem. This is how we can find the best way to resolve a school blockage without rushing and thanks to a common understanding of the situation.

I need a break

How do you hear and what does it mean to *say I need a break*? It all depends on the intonation. A call with a background of fatigue, sometimes between despair and anger, that imposes to take measures as soon as possible to counter the exhaustion in order to avoid an irreversible drop-out as it is sometimes the case in a severe *burn-out*. But we will see in the next chapter that the insistent plea *I just need a little break is a* matter of manipulating the emotional cord, often maternal. Of course, this deserves to be considered as well, but by untangling the part of suffering and staging in order to save oneself the effort and to escape the obstacle.

Rose, a studious and perfectionist student, has so far hidden her anxiety and fatigue, more overwhelmed by what she imposes on herself than by the amount of work she does. She also hides her difficulties, not wanting to appear foolish in the eyes of her parents and the other students. The hours spent understanding, highlighting and revising have eaten into her sleep. The parents see her getting tired, but they think she wants to do well and that reassures them. Results are very important to them. They want her to get into a prestigious high school, saying that it's for her own good and that she wants it too. So Rose does everything she can not to disappoint them, and has done so since elementary school, because she is afraid of not being loved anymore, of being rejected if she does not fulfill her mission: to carry the family name high. It is as if she had to pay a debt to her parents, who were so attentive and kind to her: this is what she expressed during her first consultation with me, feeling guilty for not living up to their expectations.

Her parents and her, linked in their objectives, have placed a major stake in school. But it has gone too far, and she can no longer hide her exhaustion and the suffering that assails her to the point of not being able to concentrate and lose sleep. It is already very late when she dares to tell them: *I need a break.* Contrary to what she had feared, the parents agreed in principle, at least for a week. But of course, the week passed and it was impossible for Rose to mobilize again. She goes from her bed to the cupboard with cakes and mortifies herself not to be able to return in class and to nibble unceasingly. The tension rises, the parents are impatient, they do not understand their daughter's attitude. The remarks were flying: *You are already fat enough as it is, it is not like that that you will succeed in being selected for Saint-Louis,* which plunges a little more Rose in distress. What had to happen happened, after three weeks of being taken out of school, she swallowed some medication with the idea of ending her life, but also to alert her parents to her distress and to look for a respite, which she found during a short hospitalization that finally allowed her parents to become aware of the seriousness of her condition.

It is in this context that I receive her, with a one month renewable sick leave. What can I say? The parents accepted a week's rest but they did not understand the meaning of *I need a break*, timidly pronounced by Rose, begging them, without wanting to show that she was breaking down. It is very unfortunate that she came so close to suicide to be heard. It is also unfortunate that they were not attentive to their daughter's difficulties and exhaustion, seeing only the promise of an elite career. Worse, they led her to believe that it was only her desire when, since early childhood, she had been working hard just to satisfy her parents' vicarious thirst for success. Although she had managed to obtain diplomas and a rather satisfying job, the father, hoping for more, envied his superiors. He repeats to his daughter: *"If you do well, you won't have a boss on your back"*, which sets the tone of his bitterness and traces Rose's obligatory path. The mother is employed in the retail industry. She adds: *"Above all, don't do like me, you must succeed at all costs, even if you have difficulty.* During the psychotherapy sessions, Rose tells me these words that are engraved in her brain like marble. Saying them allows her to try to detach herself from these injunctions that are at the origin of her perfectionism. But at the same time, these recommendations put up a wall that holds her back, implying that *if you are like us, if you don't look like us, you won't be able to live up to our expectations.*

In Rose's situation, the really good solution, after her suicide attempt, is to rest as long as necessary, and then have psychotherapy. This will allow her to free herself from these explicit and implicit injunctions which have vectored her desire according to that of her parents, made up of bitterness, unhealthy envy, resentment, because they have not succeeded as they hoped. Their speech *we do the maximum for her, we only want her good* mask *she must succeed to repair our feeling of failure, she owes us that because we did everything for her.* It is not a question of throwing stones at these parents who are not aware of what they have invested in their offspring, but of freeing them from a mission that does not belong to them. The problem is that the fold of requirement and perfectionism is taken, it is thus very difficult to release from it. As Rose says, *it's in me, I can't do otherwise, I have to be the best in the class. If I try to relax a bit, I feel guilty, I get stressed so I have to work again. Today it's not because of my parents who understood and let me free.*

It would take more than two years, with distractions, a boyfriend, and parents who asked her to go out, before Rose would allow herself to think and live her life in ways other than through school work. This does not prevent her from succeeding. On the contrary, the cognitive obstacles linked to stress and to her unconscious duality between parental desire and giving birth to her desire, were gradually lifted. The quality of attention, concentration and memory is closely linked to the capacity of the brain to be available, i.e. less encumbered by fear and contradictory emotions between guilt and aggressive revolt.

At the same time as Rose's psychotherapy, was it necessary to propose to the parents that they undergo the same exercise, individually, as a couple or in family therapy? Rose's suicide attempt was like an electric shock to them. They understood the seriousness of her condition and began to question their education. Was this enough? The evolution of the psycho-affective relationship does not depend only on the educational positions. Their resolve to make their daughter happy without burdening her with their aspirations had to be consolidated by their own growth. Rather than referring them to another therapist, as shrinks do, so as not to interfere with the child's psychotherapy with the risk of jeopardizing it, I waited until Rose was ready to offer her talks with her parents in the mode of informal family therapy. Why this choice? First of all, so that Rose could express to her parents herself what she understood and what she would like to hear from them. She does this carefully and tactfully. I listen to her, and the parents listen to her all the more attentively because my presence forces them to do so. This works well, with criticism, justifications, tears and hugs. This is how they finally discover their daughter, and this is done more quickly than by going into psychotherapy on their own. This also allowed this father to meet a psychologist at a later stage, not wanting to burden his daughter with his rather painful childhood history.

All of this would not have been possible without the information, coordination and support of Rose's teachers who played along by offering her a very flexible arrangement of her schedule and assessment constraints. This is far from always the case. The rigidity of some schools and teachers forces them to prolong the withdrawal from school at the risk of losing a school year. Of course, it is not really lost because the in-depth work of psychotherapy acts for the future and the well-being of the child, therefore for his success. But Rose's teachers' concern was ideal. The deafness of certain schools in the face of such blockages, which they would be able to soften, is not tolerable. Under the pretext of not disturbing their organization - admittedly complicated - the administration and the teachers hide behind the obligation of presence to refuse a crucial temporary arrangement when the student is in danger. Some come to threaten parents with a report if they don't bring in as soon as possible a medical justification for the child's absence when they know perfectly well that the child is in pain. This is often the reason for the first consultation with the psychiatrist and his first act is to write the medical certificate of absence. In order not to increase the anguish of the child and the parents, he often adds a request to set up a transitional adaptation to transmit the lessons at home, while insisting on calming the rhythm of work. Indeed, one must navigate between the stress of dropping out and the need for rest, depending on the level of exhaustion and anxiety. Complete rest, while sometimes essential, can exacerbate the symptoms because being too far away from class work is itself a source of anxiety for a studious student.

Rest and reconciliation were the two axes of Rose's reconstruction. The exhaustion was all the more important because it was several years old. Sitting at her desk in front of a lesson or an assignment had become a nightmare. What was true for Rose is almost generally true for any studious, perfectionist child who burns out to the point of breaking down. School *burnout* is a reality that affects children as much as adults. The cause of a student's exhaustion is sometimes more than just tyrannical demands on oneself. Cognitive or instrumental difficulties require extra effort. It can also be a question of a psychic or neuropsychic development which compromises school acquisitions, either by preventing them by an incapacity, or by delaying them by simple immaturity. Here again, the child may redouble his or her efforts without obtaining satisfactory results, either for him or for his parents, who sometimes become impatient and do not accept this deficit, even if it is transitory. Overwork, stress, the ingredients are there to make a *burn-out*. This was not the case for Rose who was not able to initiate by herself her extraction from the parental desire to go towards her adolescent maturation and the affirmation of her own desire.

I just need a little break

Everything is in the nuance: the *right* and *small* words soften the parents. The intonation in the form of a discreet supplication invites them to get closer to their *still small child* and the seductive mimicry closes the whole thing: *he cracks us up with his clownish face*. During the first consultation, the mother tells us:

"We didn't really realize it. The first time, Robin told us, *'I'm not going to school today*. He was a little sick, so we let him rest. The next day, he continued: *I can't, I'm too tired... I can't get up anymore*. After two weeks, the school was getting impatient and so were we. I took him to our doctor, who found him pale, ordered a biological check-up and a test for mononucleosis, the disease of adolescents. Everything was normal. In front of him, Robin told us: *I just need a little break*. When the doctor extended the rest for a week, he looked at us with a little smile. Since then, if we want to stimulate him to go to school, he repeats his little phrase. It's been three weeks and we can't get out of it.

After a month out of school, the mother begins to understand her son's little game while the father, who has given up caring for him, adds:

- He makes his mother work, he knows how to take it, and I have nothing to say, except that I am the whipping father. From the beginning, he's been the mother hen and he takes advantage of it. That's not the way he's going to do it.

Robin, embarrassed for a moment, starts to grimace and cry, telling his father that he doesn't understand anything and that he never takes care of him. The mother continues:

- And you give in to everything. You bought him an ATV for Christmas, a phone and a tablet for his birthday. Every time he asks you for something, you say yes.

- Yes, otherwise he'll have a fit, you've got him so used to giving everything away that now we can't get out of it," says the father.

I ask Robin what he thinks, if it is a good thing that his parents give in so easily. He bows his head and mumbles a *no* that seems to mean *yes*. Is his game just a whim? Does he really want something else, by refusing to go to school, than to avoid the effort and stay in his cocoon where everything is due to him? This is a really good question to ask oneself, to ask him and to ask his parents. Of course, we could simply say to him: *Enough of your whims, tomorrow you'll go back to school, that's the way it is and nothing else,* but, from experience, that wouldn't work. He might drag his feet back to school and not put any effort into it until the next time he tries to escape, which is always the case in these situations. Everything that was said in that first extended interview would have to be the starting point for a change, but which one?

The parents think they know their son. Robin believes that he can manipulate his parents to get what he wants, which will lead him nowhere but to avoid effort and real life. So the parents have to come out of their blindness and Robin understands that his little game serves him well and prevents him from growing. For the mother, it is difficult to accept that she has been fooled for a long time by her little darling who is not, or who is not any more, what she believed. How good it would be to be able to keep an idyllic image of this son that she does not really want to see grow up! Basically, when he is at home, she recognizes, he is all hers. As for the father, it is going to be necessary that he engages in the education of his son by accepting to stick to his crises because it is not a question any more of yielding to all, and that *to spoil* him thus takes at the same time its direction to *offer* and to *deteriorate*. To invest himself to temper the possessive maternal affect is also to let go of his serious tasks in order to privilege a father-son relationship, so important if he does not want to compromise Robin's future. The father is disillusioned and the mother disconcerted by this crisis that they will have to face.

Not being more than a few weeks away from solving a fundamental problem, I propose that Robin rest, yes, but a real rest without screens or playful activities, or outings with parents. In short, a rest to reflect and understand the impasse in which he is trapped. I might as well say that Robin does not appreciate at all my position which satisfies the father, even if he fears crises at home: *But he has already made us see so much that a little more or a little less, I accept the offer.* As for the mother, she bends with bad grace.

It is in this context of hostility that I receive Robin alone. The first moment was rather cold, he was mute, sullen.

"Deep down, what do you want? You've had your little break, and now you should go back but something scares you. Do you have any idea? Is college hard? The work, the effort, the others? Or are you afraid of growing up?

He looks at me with a babyish smile and adds:

- That's not cool, what you said to my parents. It's not their fault, it's mine: I don't want it to change. Yes, it's true, I'm afraid to grow up, but so what?

I add:

- You have a right to be afraid, and maybe you're right. More and more is being asked of a big boy, and you're finding that the adult world isn't very easy. Are you having trouble in middle school?"

He tells me that he is called a baby, a dwarf, because he is the smallest in his 5th grade class. He is afraid of the older students and

III - Should we trust the solutions found by the child?

teachers because he doesn't understand everything they say. He is stressed but doesn't want to show it. So he prefers to hide at home, but he knows that this is not the right solution. If I could keep him from going back, he'd be happy, but that's not what he's really asking for. During the interviews, I realize that he is looking for a way to take his place as a grown-up, while being convinced that he will not succeed. The maternal cocoon is his only fallback solution, but it is a trap.

Two false good solutions are effectively ruled out: neither staying home, Robin's solution, nor pushing him to return to college by depriving him of his spoiled child comfort, the solution that emerged from the parental complaint I had begun to engage in. However, it allowed Robin to express his difficulties in entering adolescence and to ask for help. While respecting medical confidentiality, I tell the father that his role is essential for Robin's evolution, making him understand that his son was waiting for a manual to grow up and face life. I suggest that he remember his teenage years and tell his son how he dealt with difficult situations, with anecdotes to boot. The idea is not to lecture his son, but to open the way for him, to give him some guidelines, words and attitudes that will help him become the young man that a father can hope to be. The message was well received and Robin went back to school with a complicity with his father that he had not known until then. Contrary to what was supposed, the mother was satisfied, far from the *preconceived notion* that she was a possessive mother who would push the father aside.

This really good solution to help him grow up was finally found. After the initial mistake, due to the appearance that Robin's attitude and the parents' words gave to think, the warm and attentive listening, essential, whatever the blocking situation, allowed Robin to reveal his uneasiness: to be the prisoner of his spoiled childhood (which means, there, *degraded*) and to perceive adolescence as an impassable wall.

Don't worry, I can handle it

Léopold, 13 years old, consults after more than three weeks of being out of school. His parents are anxious, even though their son has reassured them by minimizing the problem. *Don't worry, I can handle it"* seems to be his mother's favourite phrase, but in his situation, it doesn't hold up. By dint of insisting, he broke down, crying, the parents finally understood the reason: harassment by a group of students. They preferred to take a precautionary measure and to keep him at home while waiting for the reaction of the school. Everything seems to have been done, information and sanctions, in order to facilitate Léopold's return under good conditions, but he does not feel at all ready to go back. He is still very shocked by the insults (*faggot, faggot,* and other humiliations) and fears that it will happen again. The parents understand this, but they fear that he will ruin his chances and his school year.

Leopold asks to see me alone, which presages a rather embarrassing confidence, enough not to mention it in front of his parents.

"I think the stalkers, they don't know what they're talking about and it's not right. I'm the smallest kid in the seventh grade and to them I look like a girl. That's because I'm not very muscular and my voice hasn't changed yet. Since I don't play soccer well, they insult me: that's what middle school is all about. You can't ask too much of them. They don't know much about bullying.

I reply:

- It's true, you're pretty thin, and while your long hair is beautiful, to them it can be confusing. But, tell me, why do you defend them? It seems like you're protecting them and you're afraid to blame them for being mean to you.

Silence, he smiles at me, hesitates to start:

- It's like this, I don't like to say bad things about others. I don't know why but I need to forgive them. I prefer to be nice, and if everyone did what I do, it would be cool."

It is true, a kindness emanates from this intelligent, endearing androgynous-looking being. He exudes an empathy, a caring and an availability that unfortunately is not found in a world of bullies. He needs that, and that's why he can't go back to school.

An agreement was reached with the school, which was understanding, for a gradual return to school, moving from work at home to a more or less flexible schooling depending on Léopold's feelings. Everything went well, only in sports and group work did he not manage to integrate, but this was a small problem compared to the initial blockage of his schooling.

I suggested that the interviews be spaced out, but the very next month the father requested a new appointment and came into the office with his son, who also asked him to start talking because it was too difficult for him.

"That's it, Leopold doesn't feel like a boy. He had already talked to us about it and I had trivialized it, telling him that everyone was a boy in his own way, that he didn't need to play soccer and drive a lot of cars to be a boy, but it came back. We had a long discussion together after a movie. He told me that he wanted to be a girl, that it was possible, that it was a transition, and that he was ready to do it. As you know, my son is very smart. He thinks better than I do, and if he's telling me that, I think he knows what he's saying.

I had already noticed the relevance and intelligence of Leopold, but here I was stunned, I had missed the problem of this young man who, relieved, spoke again:

- Since I was little, I feel better with girls, I like to play with them. I have never had a fight with a girl. They are never violent, well, with me because it can be terrible between them too. So when I watched this movie, I decided to talk with my parents. I've been thinking about it since I was in middle school. That's why I understand boys, I'm not part of their clan, and I don't mind.

After thanking him for trusting me, I explained the process to him, pointing out that it is complicated, that it takes a long time and that we don't always get the expected result.

- I know all this, I've been on the forums where they explain what to do. I don't expect a miracle, I just want to feel better. I think this transition to being a girl would help me a lot. I'm telling you about it today, but it's not so that we can start the process right away. I'm in no hurry, I need my parents to get used to it and I need to feel really ready."

We agree that he comes to meet me whenever he feels like it.

A few months later, he comes back to tell me that everything is better, that he is still thinking about the transition but that he is not in any hurry and that maybe he won't even make it. In fact, he has found a group of friends who do theater. He joined them and it was a revelation for him. According to what the teacher told him, he is a good actor and plans to continue... and why not make it his profession?

The real solution in Leopold's case is the mobilization of the parents and the school, who are doing what is necessary to stop the harassment and facilitate the return of a young person they appreciate and trust. But this is not enough to erase the trauma. On the other hand, it allows Leopold to open up to his parents and his shrink about his androgynous experience, an in-between that is difficult to assume. At first, while reading on the forums the current events and the discussions around the sexual assignment, he interprets his malaise as an error of sexuation which it is a question of repairing by a transition with the assistance of the administration, which evolves in this field, and the doctors, this in order to become girl. The false good solution would have been to accede hastily to his request which, he said it himself, was not so urgent. Basically, he needed his difference to be heard and respected, to be able to live his feminine expression, which is more developed than usually in boys who have to give it up to be *guys*. Trusting his intelligence, his poise and not looking for a miracle cure for his blockage, that was the real good solution while waiting for him to discover himself, to find his marks as a teenager, which was the case thanks to the theater.

Let me go, I'll blow it up

It has been a month since Maxime was taken out of school, and if he agrees to come and see me, it is under the threat of his mother's placement because she can't stand his behavior anymore. He has taken the threat seriously, even though he defies his mother to do so. She won't be able to do it, he wants to convince himself by putting her to the test on a daily basis. Why did he drop out of school? The teachers are fed up with his arrogance and insolence. He challenges their pedagogy and tries to catch them at fault, which he is capable of doing because he puts his extraordinary intelligence at the service of this permanent challenge. Excluded for three days by the school's disciplinary council, this 14 year old has decided that he will never set foot in a school again.

It is very painful to endure the consultations with Maxime and his mother. Obnoxious, he insults her in my presence. I am aware of his little boss provocation towards him, which aims at *showing* me *his muscles*. He knows everything, he is the strongest and all the others are buffoons, sadists, dictators, including his mother and of course all the psychiatrists *who imprison people when they are not sick, and force-feed them drugs to kill them*. He wants to test me, to make me react, to create the conflict to prove himself and to prove to me that he is the strongest, the most intelligent. To fall for it would be a big mistake. I react only on the respect he owes to his mother, who doesn't dare to react and can't take it anymore when he invectives her in front of me by kicking:

"Get off me, bitch, you don't know what you're saying. I'll blow it up, you'll see the fireworks at school...all the same, you're all bums."

He has the audacity to say that he respects her while insulting her whenever she dares to speak to me. His case is reminiscent of Hugo's, whose situation I described in the chapter "I don't give a fuck, I do what I want", which ended in his relative success thanks to the CNED and an excellent educator. I might as well say that it helps me to put up with this

dirty kid who risks turning to delinquency if I don't succeed in finding
the origin of his permanent defiance towards adults. So, the false good
solution would be to subscribe to the idea of a placement that would
spare his mother and confront him with the harsh reality of social
relationships. But this would certainly ignite the revolt. So I need to
establish a relationship of trust with him so that he will leave his armor
of all-powerful warrior and reveal his true face behind the arrogance
and rejection of everything. He excludes himself, does everything to be
excluded, so I must not exclude him.

Maxime's deschooling and destructive defiance are the antithesis
of Leopold's, whose intelligence is constructive while Maxime's is in
the service of a systematic ravaging of the hierarchical relationship
as well as of the relationships with the other students he despises.
He is convinced of a fundamental injustice towards him. It is
urgent to understand the origin of this injustice before he becomes
completely isolated and his mother rejects him, which is beginning
to happen. In his state, it is unthinkable to offer him an establishment from which he will be rejected, repeating a morbid sequence
of provocation, exclusion, victimization, reinforcement of the
provocation until the exclusion which has the function of proving to
him that no other way is possible. The psychotherapy will therefore
try to dismantle this process by returning to the original injustice, or
at least experienced as such. This is the real good solution that will
be effective in the long term.

Finding a constructive outcome quickly implies both protecting
and supporting the mother so that she does not concretize a rejection
that would be fatal for Maxime. While the in-depth psychotherapy
continues and focuses, as is often the case in these situations, on a
failing and violent father figure, sessions with mother and son allow
for the exploration of the few possible paths. After much shouting and
arguments, the option was taken of a CNED course associated with a
measure of relief for his mother, presented to Maxime as positive. The
grandmother, with whom he is less aggressive, accepts that he comes to

her house during the day but on the condition that he works, which he promises with his lips. It is not necessary to ask too much of him. The bet is that he can put his intelligence at the service of knowledge and success which would allow him, as he wishes, to become a politician capable of reforming this *rotten world* which he hates for reasons he does not yet know. Let's not fear the birth of a new dictator, as long as his psychotherapy goes in the right direction.

We must accept that the real good solution is precarious and sometimes shaky, for lack of a better one. Let's start from the principle that we must always trust a pre-adolescent and his capacity to create in him a person of character who does not solve his impasses by destroying others, which is unfortunately too often the case, including in politics. The testimonies of Hitler's doctors who treated him during the First World War point in the direction (unconfirmed because Hitler had his medical archives destroyed) of a traumatic neurosis poorly treated by a behavioral therapy aiming to galvanize him in order to put him back on his feet and to consolidate his psychic wound. What had to happen happened, the galvanization resulted in his revenge in a spirit of vengeance against his sworn enemies: intelligence and success. Building an empire on the ruins of his methodical destruction of humanity was, among other things, the result of a therapeutic failure. One must never forget these extreme situations when treating a young person like Maxime who can, if one is clumsy and aggravates his exclusion, evolve very badly.

The real good solution was to avoid a frontal relationship that would feed destructiveness towards him and towards us, mother and caregiver. This does not mean accepting everything from him; among other things, he owes respect to his mother who never let him go. In the same way that we can say that if Hitler had been admitted to the Fine Arts, if we had considered his artistic fiber, none of the disaster of the Second World War and the Shoah would have happened. I have to use the only opportunity at my disposal: to reveal Maxim's creativity. What is called sublimation allows the creation of beautiful artistic works and inventions. Transforming sexual impulses and destructive impulses through creativity allows for the resolution of inner conflicts and suffering that it is beneficial, even vital, to express, but in a socially compatible and ultimately constructive form. Succeeding in his CNED course will answer for a part to this sublimation but it will not be enough because what is school sends Maxime back to the frustration of his omnipotence. He cannot find there a real outlet for the pressure of his dazzling intelligence and his aggressive impulses, the whole intermingled being at the service of the destruction of the other and of the established order. Like Leopold, he found in the theater a way of expression that he completed, at his request, by an initiation to opera singing. This astonishing choice proves its effectiveness by freeing him from his terrible impulsive pressure. It remains to trust him in his capacity to repair himself psychically.

When you stop arguing, I'll go back

Sophie, 12 years old, has refused to go to school for more than two weeks. She is afraid that she will faint and that everyone will laugh at her. She consulted the attending physician following a dizziness, followed by a fall without loss of consciousness. The workup showed nothing except a low blood pressure. Conclusion: vagal malaise at the approach of puberty, and advice: drink, eat, take vitamins but above all consult a child psychiatrist. Silent, visibly shy but well surrounded by her two imposing and voluble parents, I feel her worried. Father:

"I don't understand her, we do everything to please her and she does well in school. She has everything to be happy. In my opinion, she is either acting or hiding something from us.

Mother:

- When I ask her to get up, she gives me a fit. I can't make her decide. I don't think she wants to go to school. Is someone bothering you, honey?"

Sophie nods her head no. The mother continues to explain the case of her only daughter, who has so far posed no problems. I feel Sophie shrink and start to cry, so I ask to see her alone.

After such a strong passage, I can only hope to hear Sophie if I relax the atmosphere and show her a sympathetic concern. I tell her that her parents may not have understood what is happening to her and that I will respect medical confidentiality. *They do not stop arguing, I am afraid that they separate.* Once the situation is settled, we talk about how she came to drop out of school. Following a violent argument between her parents, she hardly slept all night while imagining that they were going to separate like her friend's parents. The next morning, she was unable to leave for school, panicking at the thought of coming home from school to find that her mother had left the house. *They often fight in the evening when my dad comes home from work. He's stressed out and yells at nothing.* She never shows her anguish because she is afraid of her mother's reaction, who gets angry as soon as things don't go her way. As a pre-teenager approaching puberty, Sophie is quite mature for her age. She reasons well, her fear is quite logical. I argue by telling her that many parents argue, that it is very unpleasant for the children, but that it is not for that reason that they separate. I add:

"You should make them understand that it's painful for you and that it should change.

Distraught, she adds:

- You can't talk to them about it, or it will be bad. They would get even more upset and they wouldn't like me anymore. One day my mom told me she would put me in a foster home, I'm too scared of that ."

The girls talk a lot during recess. It is a source of dramatization of the situations of each of them. And Sophie is inspired by the worst, the testimony of a friend who was placed in foster care following violence by her parents.

After two interviews, Sophie agrees to a family meeting on the condition that I speak because she feels unable to do so, which I do tactfully in front of attentive parents. They say that they are not ogres, but their sensitivity seems to be on edge. They listen, smiling, with glances and tender gestures towards their daughter. They reassure her that they will always be with her, that she can always count on them, that they will never separate, even if they have, they admit, dog-like characters, and that they should not argue in front of her. The father never had the idea that she could hear them. The mother can hardly hide the fact that she is at the end of her tether, glaring at her husband.

"Honey, don't worry, take it easy, we'll make sure we don't fight again.

The ambiguous nature of these words did not escape Sophie's attention. She starts to cry and then explodes:

- I know it will happen. Anyway, you can't talk without yelling, I'm sick of it. School, when you stop arguing, I'll go back, but I don't trust you anymore.

The key phrase is dropped, so much so that the father does not appreciate what he judges as a threat... and the mother adds:

- I knew you were doing this against us."

Sophie says that she can't do anything against them, that she can't help it, that it's stronger than her, that it paralyses her. She doesn't do this to annoy them but they don't seem to understand her suffering.

In fact, Sophie is traumatized by the violent arguments and fears being abandoned. It is impossible for her to leave the house. If she tries to do so, she is gripped by anxiety in her body. She remembers very well the words of her mother who got angry at her when she couldn't get up, telling her: *You don't want to piss me off either, or I'll leave and let you two work it out!* Then she slammed the front door. Sophie was convinced that she had left and left her alone. This only made the fear of losing her mother worse. At the bottom of her bed, terrorized, guilty of causing problems for her parents, as soon as she got up, she felt dizzy and could no longer eat. She would only come to my consultation. So I decided, right or wrong, to receive the parents alone in order to explain to them what a child could feel and to make them remember their own childhood. The father, having lost his

III - Should we trust the solutions found by the child?

mother, had been placed in a strict boarding school at a very young age, without affect. He admits that he still suffers from this. The mother had an abusive father and never stops comparing her husband to his father. They are made to not get along, that is to say, to accentuate their own suffering in contact with each other. *That's why we only had one child. I would like her to be happier than me. Right now, I can't take it anymore, I'm at the end of my rope.* The father seems to understand that the ball is in his court and that he has to stop getting so angry. He asked me for a calming treatment and agreed to come back to see me alone. This was finally the right solution. Not that the father was responsible for everything, but he was the only one who could get things moving without the family exploding.

Sophie quickly returned to school, accompanied by her father, who invested himself in his daughter's well-being, understanding that she was the only one who could give him what he had not had in his childhood. It is by giving what one has not received that one can obtain it. What remained was to deal with the maternal ambivalence towards her daughter who was growing up, approaching puberty, and whom she had the painful feeling of losing. Gradually, she stopped using possessive language such as *"she's having a fit," "she made me dizzy,"* indicating that she could let her grow up and detach herself, not emotionally, but possessively. The birth of her baby was a revelation for her: *These were the most beautiful moments of my life. But today, I finally managed to tell her that I love her more than anything and that I am proud that she is growing up.* Sophie is trying to leave behind her false maturity that was aimed at supporting her mother and preventing her parents from separating. She can finally allow herself to live her pre-adolescence. In her relationships, she is left with the fear of not being loved and of being left at the slightest mistake. It is the scar of her experience of abandonment that prevented her from opposing and asserting herself in front of her parents for fear of being rejected, a fear that was well founded.

It's really time for me to quit high school

When I first meet Caroline, 14 years old, she has just passed the brevet despite a chaotic year of 9th grade and multiple absences that she cannot explain. Simply, if she is not doing well, implying that she is anxious or tired or that she does not feel like it, she does not go. Her mother is the only one to take care of her, and she knows how much her daughter is capable of losing her temper if she tries to impose something on her. In view of her absenteeism, the high school she is applying to is very reluctant to accept her. I understand that I am asked to help Caroline, sad and angry, to integrate this high school, because if she despairs, it could, according to the mother who knows her well, turn into a drama.

While I expected to receive a child-king, a princess who disposes of her mother and the others, I find myself facing a young girl on the verge of tears, in great discomfort and overwhelmed by her emotions. It is not a question of a tyrannical requirement, but of a permanent overflow of her emotional sensitivity which obviously exhausts her. I know from experience that, in these situations, the difficult school career is peppered with rejections, exclusions and failures, even though the intelligence and abilities are there but cannot be used. The meeting and the exchange with Caroline are warm, and her mother is positively involved. I support her integration in the high school of her choice, insisting on the fact that she will be psychologically accompanied during her year of secondary school. She is accepted and, enthusiastic, starts her year well, at least the first few days because she soon stops ·getting up and does not work. It seems that she is still relying on her good intellectual abilities to give the impression that she is doing well. This cannot work in this demanding high school. Absence after absence, dropping out, tantrums, anxiety, her instability is exacerbated and jeopardizes her integration. The school offered several accommodations that she welcomed as a lifeline. But nothing was done, she dropped out of school completely. Psychotherapy and medication to

III - Should we trust the solutions found by the child?

calm her anxiety and impulsivity were not enough to make her want to integrate. Her dream of becoming a lawyer was slipping away. She couldn't stand it and became depressed.

Was it a good solution to respond to this request to integrate into this prestigious high school? Was there another solution? Probably a break from school to allow her to overcome her academic impasse linked to her emotional turmoil, a source of instability, uneasiness and inability to adapt and conform to the school framework. But for her and her mother, this was not an option. The break was imposed in a depressive context that allowed Caroline to open the Pandora's box that was at the origin of her emotional and sensitive nature: the early death of her father in a violent context, an interminable family conflict over the estate. She is caught in a vice between her mother and her grandparents, and suffers from it. This anger is passed on to her mother, even though she herself is also suffering from the family chaos.

In the course of the sessions, Caroline understands why she wants to become a lawyer, and that before she can do so, she will have to be her own advocate in the family violence she is experiencing. Her critical thinking skills and intelligence will be revealed through her understanding and actions to no longer be constrained by the family conflict that has become an inner conflict. This produces a fog in her head that accentuates her emotional instability. Under these conditions, she cannot adapt, despite her efforts, to the constraints of school, neither to the students nor to the teachers. *With me, it's always too much, I overflow, I get angry, I cry, that's why school is not for me. I have friends but I think I ask too much of them. As a result, they make a fuss and everyone rejects me.* She understands her trap, her life on a rollercoaster ride between enthusiasm, then an overflow of affection until she experiences abandonment that leaves her bitter, always without hope. Then she retreats to her bed, and it starts again because she manages to find new friends until the next episode. She does the same if a teacher takes her under his wing, which is not uncommon because she is relevant and personable, but if he makes a disapproving gesture, she gets into a fight with him and doesn't return to his class. Her mother is the only one she has left, but this pillar is weakened by an illness, another source of anguish for Caroline.

It's really time for me to quit high school. I'll never make it through high school. Too bad I won't be a lawyer. I'd rather start working. I'm looking after the neighbor's children and I hope to find a job as a salesgirl. This is her conclusion out of spite, rather resigned if it wasn't for the first step of the psychological reconstruction. I don't give up accompanying her to achieve a school curriculum that matches her abilities. For her, the time of care is not the time of school. She can't do both at the same time. Indeed, when the Pandora's box opens, the instability gets much worse. But I warned her, informed her of this ordeal of care for which she gave her consent. Why did she have to do this? Because this is what will allow her to find long-term stability and avoid evolving into a sickly bipolarity, a source of de-socialization and a chaotic life despite psychiatric care.

The real solution is to put school on hold and do everything possible to offer Caroline renewed hope and the ability to socialize. After dropping out of school, the accommodations, comes the time of odd jobs, source of experience in stable families that offer her another model than her own, disunited and violent. The feedback she received valued her and reinforced her ability to socialize thanks to her pride and autonomy. Yet she would be unable to conform to the normalized standards of a high school. What to think? Is the school unable to adapt to some children, or are some children de facto unsuited to school? The efforts made by the French education system to help dropouts enabled Caroline to join a micro high school, which was flexible in its requirements. She goes there for two hours every evening. She hung up with the prospect of taking her baccalaureate in two years, while keeping an original rhythm of life between baby-sitting and her friends.

When a child accumulates hypersensitivity linked to a traumatic event and destructive family conflicts, his chances of integrating into

III - Should we trust the solutions found by the child?

the demanding environment of school and in social and emotional relationships are compromised. Hypersensitivity is not an illness in itself, and even less a component of a pathology combining high intellectual potential and high sensitivity. But it is a psychosocial handicap that can become permanent if nothing is done. It is therefore necessary to transform this hypersensitivity, which is one of the functions of psychotherapy, so that it serves as an original and creative path. This implies taking the trouble to conceive models adapted to these children, and to provide ourselves with the means and training to put them into practice. It is also necessary to work on the tolerance of all to deviances, whatever they may be, except those linked to delinquency which are subject to educational and judicial measures.

For Caroline, there were no false steps on the part of the school community, which never stopped looking for accommodation solutions, but within the limits of a standardized system. Nor was there any psychiatric label applied and the heaviness of drug treatments which themselves generated a cognitive handicap linked to the side effects. There were her own structuring initiatives and the chance of a micro-college that she was able to seize thanks to her semi-professional experiences and a well conducted psychotherapy. Today, it is not certain that she still wants to become a lawyer. Instead, she is turning to childcare and psychology.

My girlfriend is at the CNED but she needs to see a shrink

Word of mouth can be an interesting source to help solve certain problems, but it can also cause formidable effects, including the imposition of false good solutions. If we add to this the truncated or falsified information from social networks, the associations lobbying for their ideology and certain media that relay them without sorting them out, we can see a phenomenon of contagion of false good solutions to real problems. This is the case in adolescence, especially concerning the so-called school phobias which cover a variety of refusals to follow a classical school curriculum. It is also the case for the current multiplication of decisions of a gender transition under the influence of fashion and lobbies. These are false good solutions to the real malaise of adolescents. This is one of the reasons why I am writing this book, in order to sort out a situation of psychological suffering at the origin of a school block and the other debatable and contestable reasons for refusal.

It is more and more frequent that a child, rather pre-adolescent or adolescent, comes to my office with a ready-made solution to his problem. Most of the time, we discuss the problem in order to understand and deepen his difficulties, and then look together for a solution without excluding a last resort to a distance learning program such as the CNED. It also happens, and this is a more worrying phenomenon, that the parents suggest this solution, which they think will be the best for their child and, in the background, for themselves. Avoidance of social relations, authority and effort, organizational ease, comfort posture of the child or the parent, ideological rejection of educational content, refusal to grow up and face the world, ostracism towards the working classes and refusal to mix, possessive parent who maintains immaturity and dependence on his or her child, holding the child hostage in a context of conflictual separation that goes as far as parental alienation and refusal of autonomy for the child. These reasons and many others can push a child, an adolescent or his parents to consult a psychiatrist with a procession of symptoms sufficiently telling for the latter, fooled by a learned and well put together staging, to willingly submit to their will. Instrumentalized, the practitioner has difficulty in finding his way because, precautionary principle obliges, any symptom somewhat alarming requires the prevention of a potential danger (traumatic anguish, suicide attempt...).

Éléonore came for a first consultation, accompanied by her mother, who described her daughter's very high anxiety levels, having just entered her final year of high school, in a school where she knew no one. Until then, she had attended a French high school abroad where, according to her mother, she was particularly anxious until she dropped out last year in a context of increasing absenteeism. Eleonore, silent, let her mother speak, her exhausting speech being the measure of the dramatization of her daughter's condition. I receive her alone in order to hear her and to understand the stakes of this blockage. She confirms her malaise, repeating the symptoms described by her mother and adding suicidal ideas. We agreed to meet her at short notice, while trying to keep her in school. In fact, in the final year of high school, the continuous assessment counts for a large part of the baccalaureate. So the choice of studies through Parcours Sup might be limited if she takes distance learning courses. After two weeks, which she describes as extremely trying, between anxiety and the impossibility of getting up, I accede to her request in view of the worsening of the symptoms. The mother thanked me by phone, took the necessary steps and asked me several times for certificates. The request made to the CNED for Eleonore is quickly accepted.

We agreed on a new appointment with Eleonore and, when the day came, no one, just a laconic text message from her mother at the last moment: *Eleonore could not come.* Since then, no more news in spite of my solicitations, fearing a serious problem for my patient. It seems that this was not the case, which led me to recall a sentence of Eleonore's that had surprised me but, anxious to deepen the cause of her anxieties and her alleged school phobia, I had not stopped there. She is the daughter of an industrial director and had told me about a certain rejection of the students of this high school with a pout that I did not want to take as contempt. She had added that she would never be salaried, unless she was an executive like her father... but rather independent. It remains to be understood what her mother's role is: either attentive to symptoms to the point of helping her daughter to grow them, or manipulative because there was talk of her leaving with her daughter in the context of a marital separation. In any case, despite my experience, I was not only instrumentalized, but deceived by a perfectly orchestrated staging. When intelligence is put at the service of perversion, it is difficult to resist.

Fortunately, this caricatured situation is rather rare, but, in an attenuated form, it is quite common to feel manipulated, not by the disguise of symptoms and their accentuation, but by the pressure of a threat to end one's life or to hurt oneself. The false good solution is to freeze the refusal, the dropout, and to put in place too early a radical solution like the CNED. One must always give oneself time to understand while tinkering, in the sense of looking for adjustments, in order to loosen the knot of anxiety without compromising school integration. But the psychiatrist often arrives at the end of the road in an already very advanced process of de-schooling that he can only observe. Hence the interest in training first line practitioners so that they do not take untimely measures and refer the child to a child psychiatrist as soon as possible. Hence the interest in not rushing into a decision so as not to compromise the development of a truly good solution, with patience and full knowledge of the causes of the problem.

*

My girlfriend is at the CNED. She told me that in order to get it, I had to meet with a shrink, that's why I came to see you, a naive statement that has the merit of being clear: make sure that I don't go to college anymore because it's too difficult for me. Jeanne describes her fear as soon as she approaches the school, to the point of panicking and freezing until her mother takes her home. Her mother does not want her daughter to suffer, but she is not at all in favor of correspondence courses. She wants Jeanne to overcome her fear and succeed in returning to the *good college where she is, where her friends are waiting for her.*

After having decided on a light anxiolytic treatment and a psychotherapy in order to understand what is happening to her, Jeanne accepts, reassured by the fact that a friend brings her the lessons and that the teachers give her the homework through Pronote, the Internet exchange software. She is well organized and actively participates in the discovery of the source of her anguish: abandonment by her father, who remarried after leaving home abruptly when she was a child, birth of a baby at the father's home, her mother's illness, harassment during her first year of college, all the more serious because she was very vulnerable, given her experience of abandonment. In short, if I may say so and unfortunately, a classic at the origin of school phobias. Little by little, she gained confidence and decided to write to her father, a firm letter to which he replied weakly. She wrote again and hit the nail on the head, comparing him to a lifeguard who would look at her drowning and smile, then walk away, leaving her for dead. From there, the father started calling her and then inviting her to his house. She wasn't ready for it, but it made her feel better about going back to school. It turned out to be more complicated than she expected and than her mother and I expected. We had to decide, for one year only, to join the CNED, which turned out to be a really good solution in view of her work and organization skills. We also decided to do this because the repair of trauma could be done all the better if we did not take the premature risk of experiencing microaggressions like she was likely to experience, still fragile, in her school.

*

If the difference between the situations of Éléonore and Jeanne is obvious, it is first of all linked to my lack of vigilance and my mistake in the first case. It is also linked to the fact that Jeanne, fragile and naive, always remained simple and authentic. She did not hesitate when faced with the offer of care, which she knew how to make the most of. And after a year at the CNED, she resumed a classical curriculum, supported by her friends. Today, she is better, without needing to see her father again; she only needs to talk to him when he contacts her, quite regularly.

I Don't Want to Go to School Anymore

I want to stay at home, you'll teach me

It is not uncommon for a child entering the first grade to be destabilized and to develop anxious manifestations, mainly of a somatic nature: stomach aches, nausea and dizziness in a context of motor inhibition and sadness. Most often, with patience and attention, the habit is acquired and the symptoms are resolved. For some children who have often experienced these anxious manifestations at the beginning of each school year in kindergarten, the situation worsens over time until it becomes impossible to return to school. This was the case for Paul, 7 years old, when he consulted us after several weeks of being taken out of school. Separating from his mother has always been difficult for him... and for her who, paradoxically but frequently, wants him to grow up and become her *little man*, she says while looking at him warmly. He slept in his parents' bed until he was 4 years old, because he was very anxious at night, preventing everyone from sleeping, including the inhabitants of the building, a source of a neighborhood problem. Even now, and even more so since he started first grade, he joins them in their bed because he is very afraid despite his nightlight and the door ajar. While his mother talks about his situation, he sticks to her, takes his thumb and turns his back to me. The mass is said: *I will not leave mom.*

Connecting with a child who is regressively withdrawn into his mother's lap requires patience and humor to the point of taking a place in his safety perimeter. There is no point in being authoritative and trying to forcefully separate the mother from her child. They are intimately involved, out of emotional immaturity and insecurity for him, out of love and necessity for the mother who does not want to see him suffer or create a family disruption. Everything foreign constitutes a danger for Paul, so the school of course, but also the shrink who is talking about his case with his mother. He thinks: *What will happen, what will he do to me?* So he seeks protection from her.

Paul is a big baby, a bit clumsy, fond of cakes, still very much in an oral phase of his psychic development. His mother knew that he was nicknamed *Kinder Bueno* in the school playground, after the candy whose shameless publicity is equal to its harmful components. It took Paul a while to realize that this meant he was fat. This only reinforced the threat posed by the other students, even more so than the teacher.

The situation seems to be blocked, and I propose not to focus on school and to accept this moment of unschooling in order to help Paul in this stage of emotional separation. The mother, having taken parental leave when a little girl was born, accepts the principle, especially since Paul, who has welcomed his sister, has nevertheless shown signs of infantile regression since this event, which separates him a little from his mother. It remains for me to do this work, which is quite usual, to make sure that the father-son relationship is privileged in order to gently untie the mother-son fusional link. But Paul doesn't see it that way. For him, staying at home must allow him to strengthen his maternal bond and he is not at all happy about having activities with his father. When his father intervenes, he places him among the intruders, those who disturb and put him in psycho-affective danger.

"I want to stay home and have you teach me," he whispers to his mother, looking at me out of the corner of his eye.

This one repeats it to me, adding:

- You see how he is with me. At home, I can't do anything, he's always glued to me."

He makes it clear to me that he will not let go of his hegemonic position easily. If it were simple, the parents could have resolved this emotional stage of Paul's life by themselves. Indeed, it is neither a whim nor a tyranny that he is exercising over his parents, especially his mother, even though it looks like it. He is simply not ready to take that step of emotional detachment that opens him up to society, the first step of which for Paul was school. Indeed, until the age of 3, his mother and maternal grandmother took care of him with only a few forays into the playground. Therefore, if he is forced to go to school, this trauma is likely to continue throughout his schooling, and even throughout his life, with a tendency to withdraw, psychomotor inhibition and a deficit of attention and concentration that are very troublesome for school learning, professional integration and social relations.

Three months were enough to get through this stage. It is sometimes more, rarely less, in these quite frequent situations and finally quite simple to unravel if one goes about it tactfully and gently. I insist on the necessity of this break without force to enter the school. If school is important for both learning and socialization, no one can deny it, it is necessary to enter under good conditions in order to take full advantage of the contributions it allows. A judicious approach makes it possible to establish a pleasure to go to school, to join friends, to open one's cognitive capacities (memory, attention, concentration), in a climate of security and valorization. This is the real good solution, even if it does not always please the family or the school, for whom the child must follow standard stages according to age, defined by a normative psychology, now supported by neuropsychology, which is ready to declare a handicap if there is any cognitive or behavioral discrepancy.

I promise to go back

It's quite gratifying to hear your child who has been out of school for several weeks, or even months, say that he or she feels ready, or at least that he or she is going back. You tell yourself that things are getting better, which is often the reality after a rest, quality exchanges with the parents and psychotherapeutic follow-up. If the difficulties and the anxiety have calmed down, the return to school is never easy. It is an achievement that requires special attention and the temporary reinforcement of follow-up to avoid a relapse. The child must find his place again. He or she will have to answer questions from friends and others, and get back up to speed on school skills. This challenge can backfire if a mass of obstacles crushes him without his being supported or encouraged. It is an enormous effort that is more often motivated by fear of disappointing parents, losing friends, and increasing isolation than by a real need to return to school. Pride and pleasure will come a little later. At the beginning, it is the pressure of an obligation linked to the worried entourage and the feeling of guilt. It can also be, in the situation of unschooling for comfort, to lose this comfort thanks to the skill of parents who do not make life too easy for their child.

I promise you, I will go back, were the words that Katia, 15 years old, pronounced in front of the pressure of her parents who were worried about her dropping out of school since two months. The next morning, to her mother's astonishment, she left, relaxed, for high school but did not return that evening. After checking with one of her friends, she didn't show up at school. The alarm was raised, the parents searched for her and phoned her friends. They were worried and feared the worst. The police mobilized the next day and found her prostrate and hypothermic on the steps of an abandoned house... a night in the emergency room, a visit from the psychiatrist on duty and a discharge the next day at her request and that of her parents who promised to have her followed by a child psychiatrist.

It is in this anxious context that I receive Katia for the first time, surrounded by her parents. I am astonished that in two months of being out of school, she has not consulted a child psychiatrist. The mother tells that she is followed by the attending physician who prescribed an anxiolytic, but did not propose a specialized consultation. She states:

"In the family, we're not much for shrinks, so he's tried to talk to her and so have we, but she won't say anything.

The father adds:

- Our main concern was that she would miss high school. We must have missed the problem. She locks herself away and spends all her time in her room. If we come to see her, she refuses to talk to us."

I shorten this interview to meet Katia before she closes. *It's not worth it with them, they don't want to understand. All they want is for me to go to school. They don't care that I'm not in good spirits. They keep saying that I'm going to fail, that I'm going to flunk, that I can't do it, that they're going to work, so why shouldn't I? They took away my phone and forbid me to go out until I go back to school. Anyway, I don't want to go out, I just want to die.* Katia cries, while saying that she understands them, that she sucks, that she is ashamed of herself, that she never wanted to disappoint them, but it is stronger than her. So she went back to school to stop it, but she knew when she left that she wasn't going. She had taken all her medication to kill herself. After swallowing them, she went to a place where she thought no one would find her. Depressed and suicidal for several weeks, Katia was in great danger. Considering the delay of hospitalization, on a waiting list of one month, I propose an intensive psychotherapy with a daily relay by email in order to answer her request to confide her distress. After describing her feelings of suffering, her submission to the demands of her parents, I understood how the chosen solution had been the worst one: pressuring her to return to school at all costs and lecturing her by threatening her. No one could or would really listen to her. The parents questioned her without wanting to hear her suffering. The attending physician spoke more with the mother than with her. They kept telling her: *"If you want to get out of this, you'll have to work, that's what we've done all our lives, so make an effort. It's not much, what we're asking of you.*

Nothing like this to make Katia feel guilty and to aggravate her depression, which leads to shame and self-rejection. But this did not answer the question: why this impossibility to go to school until the dead end of suicide rather than going there? It was necessary to establish a solid trust so that Katia could tell the painful dilemma in which she found herself between the pressure of her parents' school work, the normative pressure of the high school, and the demands of a girl in her class who had become her love interest in the greatest secrecy. Her friend wanted Katia to tell her parents about it, an unthinkable challenge that was the source of her anxiety and sense of guilt, as Katia was caught in a conflict of loyalties between her parents and her friend. The anxiety was at its peak when the latter threatened to leave her if she did not comply, thus taking advantage of her hold on Katia whose first relationship was tinged with dependence and guilt. Katia had to flee the school to avoid seeing her and try to get rid of her. It was just as unbearable to find herself in front of her parents, hence her isolation in her room to brood over this trap. From anguish to depression and then to the solution of suicide, it was for her the best and only solution: to disappear to escape her friend and her feeling of guilt, which really almost happened.

If the parents, while remaining discreet and attentive, contacted me to improve communication with their daughter, the question that was burning in their minds was: *When will she be able to return to school?* Without betraying any medical secrecy, I encouraged them to talk about something else with their daughter. On the other hand, I encouraged her to talk with them about what was bothering her because the mother had told me that she had read her daughter's diary. They were scattered notes, coded, that she had not been able to decipher but which made her think that her daughter was caught in a cult. The gap was widening, risking to lead her mother to untimely actions. So I told Katia about it. After the rage of learning that her mother had gone through her things and read her well-hidden diary, she finally agreed to talk to her, alone... with her father, no way.

At the next session, rage gave way to sadness as his mother's first reaction was:

"So I won't have a grandchild? You are my only daughter and your big brother is in China and only thinks about work. You can't do this to me, my daughter.

Later, she had returned with an apology, adding:

- I know it happens between girls, but are you sure, have you thought this through? You should talk to your shrink about it, he could fix it."

The result was catastrophic, the suicidal thoughts and self-mutilations started again. Her mother came back to the charge, proposing to change school, to leave far from this girl who *spoiled her life.* Katia jumped at the chance to ask to go to boarding school. I knew that this was a very bad solution, the risk being that she would withdraw even more into herself and that she would really end up committing suicide.

Together we looked for another solution, which we found with a crazy aunt whom Katia loved very much but whom her mother did not appreciate at all. This one was difficult to convince but, she said, *if it would make things better and get her away from this lesbian and her affinity for girls, I am ready to accept that for her*. The psychotherapy was going to continue on video. It seemed to me the best solution to rebuild herself far from her parents and far from her tyrannical friend, but without being alone, with another viewpoint that I hoped would be constructive. An arrangement with her high school made it possible not to compromise her studies and, finally, she left until the end of the school year. This peace of mind, far from all her worries, allowed her to separate from her friend who weighed too much on her and on her guilty conscience, while asserting herself in front of her parents thanks to the support of her aunt.

In fact, the best solution was to allow her to really engage in her adolescence by leaving the parental yoke without breaking, by asserting herself in front of them as well as in front of the others. The resumption of school work, associated with the numerous distractions that her aunt proposed to her, allowed Katia to focus on the search for her desire by untying herself from that of her parents (to be a good student in order to be a good girl and, above all, not to disappoint them) and from that of her friend who wanted to establish a couple relationship in the sight of all, in particular of her parents, which she was not ready for. Katia does not know towards whom her attraction goes, girls or boys, girls and boys. She wants to give herself time to discover life and free her desire. In fact, she has freed her head, available again, and not only for the school thing. She has just returned to her high school, and has signed up for sports and cultural activities, carefully avoiding romantic involvement because she thinks it's too early, that there are so many things to discover. She doesn't want anyone to stop her. Her parents are getting to know her, respecting her life and her desire. Her mother refrains from asking questions, understanding that wanting to talk to her daughter is first of all creating the conditions for her to want to talk to her.

I want to go to college

Marco has just spent his last two years of elementary school at home thanks to the CNED. Indeed, in third grade, he experienced harassment and physical violence. The traumatic anxiety was such that it was impossible for him to go through the school gates despite the help and patience of his mother and teacher. He immediately came for counselling. Given his high anxiety level, I had to prescribe him an anxiolytic for the first month and engage in psychotherapy focused on the violence he had suffered. For a long time he remained terrorized and paralyzed in his physical and verbal expression. The shock was all the more violent because, according to his mother, and this was confirmed, he was particularly vulnerable. Stalkers more often attack fragile, reserved, different children, those who do not play soccer and do not like fighting, which was the case of Marco, immature, very close to his mother and having not known any adversity until then either at school or in family life. He does not know his father, who left without leaving an address before the birth of this boy whom he refused to recognize.

Very studious, he succeeded perfectly in his two years of home schooling, supported by his mother, but seeking autonomy in his work and daily tasks. He asserted himself in a singular way. With me, he refused more and more to talk about things that make him angry and sad. This is understandable because he wanted to be positive and conquering, a little aggressive as soon as I didn't go his way, but more violent with his mother if she dared to upset him. On the other hand, he continued to shun social relationships. Agoraphobic, he would get upset because of his anxiety, as soon as he was pushed to go out.

During the fifth grade, he told us that he had decided to enter college in the sixth grade. Surprisingly, his mother mobilized to prevent him from going to the local high school, which was known for its violence. A very positive contact was made with a high level private school, both strict and open to differences, with a will to include children in difficulty by giving them the means. This meant that special arrangements and follow-up were ready to be put in place as soon as Marco arrived. In other words, he was expected. But he set his conditions: *I don't want any accommodation, I want to be like the others, I don't want anyone to bother me.* So it was agreed to integrate him as a *child like the others,* with the hope that it would work. I must admit that I was rather worried because the mistrust and fear of others had not disappeared, despite significant progress. But there was no other way but to trust him, which seemed to be the real way. His mother needed to have hope with him, so I didn't interfere with that.

A few days later, he complains that a child is bothering him. His mother reassures him and promises to talk about it with his main teacher. The latter, understanding, mobilizes around Marco and calls to order the child who would have harassed him. The latter complains about Marco's violence for a wrong word, a disproportionate reaction. The situation will quickly deteriorate. Each word, each gesture, Marco interprets it as an aggression. An infernal spiral starts. The more he reacts violently, the more remarks he receives, up to the threat of punishment, which he finds very unfair. He wants his mother to intervene, which she does every day, while perceiving the trap in which her son is sinking until he can no longer attend college. He demands reparation for these injustices before returning to school. The decision of the pedagogical team is going to put the fire to the powder keg, by posing as a condition to Marco's return that he accepts the presence of an AESH at his side and that the extracurricular time, notably the canteen, is suppressed. I receive Marco and his mother on many occasions, and note his violence more and more marked as well in his words as in this hostile glance towards me and towards his totally distraught mother.

The situation is blocked, we are heading towards a return to the CNED, but Marco refuses this perspective, just as he refuses to question himself. He can only see himself as a victim of the students and teachers who have plotted against him. It is not uncommon that, in the aftermath of a trauma, the systematic posture of victim leads to a persecution syndrome that spreads to all areas of life. This is the first conclusion that comes to my mind concerning him. It is to forget what his difference, his vulnerability, his agoraphobia, in particular an atypical disorder on an autistic and persecutory register, can raise.

Would the real solution have been to identify this potential disorder, masked by the traumatic situation, from the first consultations? The latter occupied the field with symptoms specific to autism but also common to it: mutism, fear, paralysis of social relations. Marco's history, his difference and his vulnerability did not plead in favor of such a disorder, but rather of a wounded immaturity. The positive evolution confirmed this, even if there were some worrying signs, notably the violence towards his mother and his emotional coldness, which was confirmed during consultations. But, after all, his demands could be considered legitimate: to be like the others so as not to be stigmatized and to make his way without being noticed, hoping to integrate and make friends. The rest can also be explained in this way: a hurtful remark, which he was dreading, set off the fire. Instead of withdrawing into his suffering, he went to the front line in an aggressive way. *A priori,* there is no reason to regret having accepted his choice, it was necessary, but the new situation is extremely problematic.

Here we are with this hesitation about the right solution. Of course, it is impossible for him to return to school. He will have to accept a return to the CNED curriculum until he gets better, which his mother and I hope he will do, so that he can resume his place in society, if not at school. The persecution syndrome that appeared obliges us to evoke together the diagnosis of a pathology intertwined between trauma and autistic disorder. Everything is a sign of aggression for him. He feels constantly humiliated and develops an aggressive anger towards everyone, including his mother. He judges her, considers that she does not defend him and that she is an accomplice of the school. As for me, he doesn't talk to me much, doesn't want anyone to think he's crazy, which he feels deep down. The empathy of all towards him was not enough to allow him to integrate into the school which, although imperfect, remained open despite the problem linked to Marco's behavior.

Sometimes, reintegration into school after a situation of harassment is complicated by the impossibility of inclusion for several reasons: intolerance of the school, renewed harassment, aggressive attitude of the parents or phobia of the child. In Marco's case, the fault does not lie with the school, which did the right thing, but with an obstacle that interferes with Marco's socialization. A pre-existing disorder went unnoticed. It was revealed *afterwards*, aggravated by the trauma. It is a double punishment for Marco who, at present, hides his despair behind his violent claims. These are legitimate, not because he would be a victim of harassment again but because the past harassment has compromised his chances of socialization. At present, he is unable to find a way to integrate into school life, even if he is protected from the ordinary violence common to all schools. It remains to help him to rebuild himself through psychotherapy and a social empowerment approach within the framework of a group of children without which his socialization will not be possible.

WHAT TO CONCLUDE BUT TO PROPOSE?

Over the course of the chapters, we have been able to grasp the various reasons for this aggravation of the phenomenon of school refusal. If it has been accentuated by the disruption of our habits following the confinement, it also corresponds to a more profound change in the relationship of children and adolescents with school obligations, effort, social promiscuity, authority, but above all the relationship to oneself, to one's image and to addictive pleasure. By comfort, by opportunism, children, especially teenagers, including with the complicity of some parents, refuse to submit to a school curriculum within an institution. It is not a question of anxious refusal or of dropping out because of failure, but of a choice. Is it a choice by default, by inability to project oneself into this radiant future of progress that we can no longer sell to the youth? Is it a real choice to no longer accept constraint and to restore pleasure as the first principle that prevails over any obligation, including that of reality which requires access to autonomy? This evolution should not be confused with cases of impossibility to enter the school or the classroom, of anxiety, of exhaustion linked to pedagogy under performance pressure. In these cases, it is not a question of choice on the part of the child or the parents but of dismay, of powerlessness in the face of what is suffered in anguish, guilt and shame. The frustration is all the greater because the proposals for alternative schooling are most often inaccessible or absent. The promising declarations of setting up the Apadhe are not really concretized. As is often the case, Peter is undressed to dress Paul, thus avoiding additional expenses. As a result, human and material resources and training are lacking. So we give up, for example, the Rased, the network of specialized help for pupils in difficulty, which had however proved its efficiency.

The communication of the school and its teachers with the child and his/her parents is increasingly marked by mistrust and misunderstanding. Similarly, unprepared and chaotic school inclusion causes painful situations that are conducive to anxious school refusal and to a withdrawal decided by the parents to protect the child from institutional and pedagogical failures. The out-of-school relays, which are beneficial, are full, especially the places in medical-educational institutes, which are lacking because of a policy of drastic savings under the pretext of inclusion in a so-called normal environment, which we know is unrealistic for children in great difficulty suffering in a school environment that is not adapted to their situation. If we add to this the fact that alternative schools and pedagogies are prevented or strangled by the constraints imposed under the pretext of security and pedagogical diktats of the National Education, the solutions become very limited.

However, we shall see, in the following chapter on useful information, that everything is there, available, rich in various proposals which have proved their worth. All that is needed is the means and the creativity, and therefore to free oneself from the ideological shackles coupled with the evaluation madness of the decision-makers and pedagogues of the National Education. Of course, not everything can be thrown away, but the solutions often come from the creative initiatives of certain schools and the energy deployed by teachers committed to working with their students in difficulty. The facts show that when it comes to planning and adapting to individual situations, the number one enemy is standardization, normalization and rigid bureaucracy. If the individualized reception project, PAI, is a happy initiative, its drafting must really take into account the difficulties of the child and the possibility of applying the device, otherwise, as I see too often, the confusion of the child and the parents deepens, full of bitterness. You only have to read the comments on forums and social networks dedicated to school phobia to see this.

If there were only one proposal to retain, it would be to give a real initiative to teachers to make their pedagogy attractive, adapted to our time. This implies loosening the stranglehold of permanent evaluation and the race for performance with the permanent threat of imposed guidance due to the alleged deficiency of the child. This implies giving teachers and students more time, in particular by drawing inspiration from the Scandinavian and German models: reorganization of the timetable and reduction of work imposed at home. Currently, some middle and high school students spend two to three hours at home in the evening, after the day's classes and the bus rides home at 7 p.m. and picks them up again at 6:30 a.m. No employee would accept to be imposed this stakhanovist regime.

If the stranglehold is loosened, with greater availability and a real easing of pedagogical pressure, it becomes possible to propose class group projects and partnerships with civil society in order to make teaching more concrete and in touch with the world. In other words, school refusal, whether anxious or opportunistic, will only be reduced if teaching is made attractive, participative and creative. To this must be added a careful watch against stigmatization, harassment, in short, the concretization of civic inclusion in the respect of the rights and duties of the child. We do not leave a student out in the cold because he or she has difficulties, or left to be preyed upon by bullies and harpies. Teachers and school administrators have to take care of this, including by disassociating themselves from a teacher who practices humiliation with his designated heads, who "bleaches" sadistically, knowing full well that the continuous assessment in the form of a sword of Damocles will compromise the future of students who are nevertheless studious.

FIND ALL THE USEFUL INFORMATION

Legislation and school obligation

Since the law of March 28, 1882, which aimed to make elementary school compulsory, secular and republican, the numerous revisions of which this law has been the subject have only aimed to improve the principle of equal opportunity in a social-republican spirit. The latest revisions of the Education Code in 2013 and 2019, and then Article 49 of the Penal Code relating to family instruction (IEF) have increased the requirements (reason for withdrawal to the family, monitoring of dropouts, control of the quality of education). The goal is to maintain schooling, regardless of the place and the pedagogy, by referring it in a compulsory way to a common base of knowledge, skills, culture but also citizenship. Indeed, freedom is not to do what you want, how you want and when you want. This freedom requires respect for the law and for others, but also the ability to be autonomous and to provide for one's needs and leisure activities. There is compulsory education from the age of 3 to 16 and compulsory training from 16 to 18. As for equality, in the social reality, it proves to be a delusion. Indeed, it is not only the law that decides this but mainly political and economic choices.

If many decrees and measures aim at equity in access to a common base of knowledge, the diversity of social and cultural conditions with its blatant inequalities and injustices are reflected in the disparity in educational achievements and the absenteeism rate. As far as dropping out without a diploma is concerned, the sad record belongs to the so-called disadvantaged and ghettoized population. What remains is fraternity, a value that requires, first and foremost, respect for others and their social, cultural and spiritual differences. Respect for secularism and freedom of expression is the guarantee of this, and empathy is the lubricant.

The exacerbation of communal withdrawals and defiant postures that are a form of terrorism challenge and endanger the founding principles of the republic and of democracy. The latest adjustments to the law aim to fight against defiance and separatism in the face of secular education, which is not immune to the effects of terror and its threats on teachers and students alike.

Let's summarize the different devices and measures of these laws:

Parents are responsible for their child's schooling, but they can choose whether to send their child to public, private or home school. The requirement is that the child masters the common base of knowledge at the end of schooling, if possible in each cycle: kindergarten, primary, secondary. School is compulsory from the age of 3 up to and including 16. Between the ages of 16 and 18, teenagers are obliged to take training, without having to follow a school curriculum. The local missions provide training assistance and monitor the young person's compliance with this obligation.

When parents decide that their child will be taught at home, the mayor of the city is obliged to investigate and monitor the terms of this curriculum in order to prevent all kinds of abuses aimed at avoiding school instruction that complies with the common base of knowledge[5]

---

5. https://www.education.gouv.fr/le-socle-commun-de-connaissances-de-competences-et-de-culture-12512

(all the knowledge, skills, values and attitudes necessary to succeed in school and in life as an individual and future citizen). The mastery of the base is necessary to obtain the national diploma of the patent.

The mayor's investigation and the controls make it possible to inform the academic director of the national education services (Dasen) of possible abuses. In the case of home schooling, it is necessary to justify the reasons and to ask for the authorization of the Dasen who requires every year a pedagogical control of the instruction brought to the child (in fact, considering the lack of means, these controls are not numerous).

What are the reasons for IEF that are accepted? A health problem, a handicap of the child, intensive sports or artistic practice, family homelessness in France, distance from any public school, but also if the physical, psychological or moral integrity of the child is threatened within his school. The pedagogical control ensures that the child has acquired the knowledge of the common base in relation to the objectives of knowledge and skills required for each cycle of education. It includes an interview with the instructors (parents or others). It must establish and prove the written and oral work done by the child.

A child enrolled in a school must attend classes according to the timetable. Absences are authorized on the condition that the school is informed and sanctioned if necessary. The child's illness, contagious disease, family events, transportation problems, and essential family travel outside of the school vacations are valid reasons for absence, provided that they are reported and justified.

Between the ages of 16 and 18, dropping out of school leaves minors to fend for themselves without having acquired any training or job prospects. The risk of social stagnation and delinquency is real. The counselors of the local missions accompany these young people in their job search and training. They are also in charge of ensuring that the training obligation is respected in conjunction with resource institutions (information and orientation centers - CIOs -, employment

Find all the useful information

centers, traditional schools or schools that help young people get back on track, such as micro-schools, second chance schools, etc.).

Excerpts from the Education Code pertaining to the July 26, 2019 law [6]

"Education is compulsory for every child from the age of 3 until the age of 16. This compulsory education is provided primarily in educational institutions. Compulsory education may be provided either in public or private institutions or schools, or in families by the parents, or one of them, or any person of their choice."

"Within the framework of the public education service and in order to contribute to its missions, a public service for digital education and distance learning is organized in order to, in particular:

1° to provide schools and educational establishments with a diversified range of digital services to extend the range of courses taught there, to enrich teaching methods and to facilitate the implementation of personalized assistance for all students;

2° to offer teachers a diversified range of educational resources, content and services contributing to their training as well as tools for monitoring their students and communicating with their families;

(3) provide instruction for children who cannot be educated in a school or educational institution, including those with special educational needs. Adapted digital media may be provided based on the specific needs of the student;

4° to contribute to the development of innovative projects and educational experiments promoting the use of digital technology in schools and cooperation.

Within the framework of this public service, the determination of the choice of resources used shall take into account the availability of free software and open format documents, if available."

---

66. https://www.legifrance.gouv.fr/codes/section_lc/LEGITEXT000006071191/LEGISCTA000006166564/2020-10-02

"When a child is temporarily absent from class, the person(s) in charge must, without delay, inform the principal of the reasons for the absence. The only reasons considered legitimate are the following: illness of the child, communicable or contagious illness of a family member, family reunion, impediment resulting from accidental communication difficulties, temporary absence of the responsible persons when the children follow them. The other reasons are assessed by the competent State authority in matters of education. The latter may consult the social workers approved by it, and instruct them to conduct an investigation, with regard to the children in question."

"The director of the educational institution shall refer the matter to the State authority competent in matters of education so that it may issue a warning to the persons responsible for the child, reminding them of the applicable criminal penalties and informing them of the parental support mechanisms available to them:

(1) when, despite the invitation of the principal of the educational institution, they have not made known the reasons for the child's absence or have given incorrect reasons for the absence;

(2) when the child has missed at least four half-days of school during the month without legitimate reason or valid excuse.

In the event of persistent non-attendance, the head of the educational establishment shall bring together the members of the educational community concerned, within the meaning of article L. 11-3, in order to offer the persons responsible for the child appropriate assistance and support, in accordance with the contract. A referral staff member is designated to monitor the measures implemented within the educational establishment."

"The school principal informs the local authorities and the authorities concerned with child protection of the measures taken in the school to combat truancy and school dropout. He or she shall be the contact person for these communities and authorities and shall be informed, in return, of the support available to him or her in order to carry out the tasks of accompanying the persons responsible for the child and preventing absenteeism."

"The State authority responsible for education may, at the request of the child's legal guardians and after the opinion of the school director has been obtained in the context of a dialogue with the educational team, authorize an adjustment of the time spent in kindergarten by children enrolled in the early childhood section, under the conditions defined by decree."

"Children subject to compulsory schooling who receive instruction in their families, including enrollment in a distance learning institution, shall from the first year, and every two years, be the subject of an investigation by the competent town hall, solely for the purpose of establishing the reasons alleged by the persons responsible for the child, and whether they are being given instruction to the extent compatible with their state of health and the family's living conditions. The result of such investigation shall be communicated to the state educational authority and to the persons responsible for the child. When the investigation has not been carried out, it shall be carried out by the representative of the State in the department. The State authority responsible for education must, at least once a year, from the third month following the declaration of instruction by the persons responsible for the child as provided for in the first paragraph of article L. 131-5, have it verified, on the one hand, that the instruction provided in the same home is provided for the children of a single family and, on the other hand, that the instruction provided complies with the child's right to instruction as defined in article L. 131-1-1. To this end, this control makes it possible to ensure the progressive acquisition by the child of each of the fields of the common base of knowledge, competences and culture defined in article L. 122-1-1 with regard to the objectives of knowledge and competences expected at the end of each cycle of teaching of the compulsory schooling. It is adapted to the child's age and, when the child has a disability or disabling health condition, to his or her particular needs.

"The control is prescribed by the State authority competent in matters of education according to modalities that it determines. It is organized in principle at the home where the child is educated. The persons responsible for the child are informed, following the annual declaration that they are required to make pursuant to the first paragraph of article L. 131-5, of the purpose and methods of the checks that will be carried out pursuant to this article. This control is carried out without delay in the event of failure to declare instruction in the family by the persons responsible for the child, without prejudice to the application of penal sanctions. The results of the control are notified to the persons responsible for the child. If the results are judged insufficient, the persons responsible for the child are informed of the deadline for a second test and of the shortcomings of the education provided that need to be remedied. They are also informed of the sanctions to which they may be subject, at the end of the procedure, pursuant to the first paragraph of article 227-17-1 of the Penal Code. If the results of the second inspection are deemed insufficient, the State authority responsible for education shall give formal notice to the persons responsible for the child to enroll him or her in a public or private school within fifteen days of being notified of the formal notice and to inform the mayor, who shall inform the State authority responsible for education, of the school or establishment they have chosen. The persons responsible for the child who have been given formal notice are obliged to enrol the child in a public or private educational establishment at least until the end of the school year following the year in which they were notified of the formal notice. When the persons responsible for the child have refused, without legitimate reason, to submit their child to the annual control provided for in the third paragraph of this article, they are informed that in the event of a second refusal, without legitimate reason, the State authority competent in matters of education is entitled to give them formal notice to enrol their child in a public or private educational establishment under the conditions and according to the methods provided for in the seventh paragraph. They shall also be notified of the sanctions to which they may be subject, at the end of the procedure, pursuant to the first paragraph of Article 227-17-1 of the Penal Code. "Art. 227-17-1. The fact, by the parents of a child or any person exercising parental authority or de facto authority over him or her on a continuous basis, of not enrolling the child in an educational establishment, without a valid excuse, despite a formal notice from the State authority competent in matters of education, is punishable by six months' imprisonment and a fine of 7,500 euros."

Provisions relating to family instruction in the Act of August 24, 2021, reinforcing respect for the principles of the Republic. Article 49[7]

"The existence of a situation specific to the child motivating the educational project, provided that the persons responsible for the child can justify the ability of the person or persons in charge of the child's education to provide family instruction in accordance with the best interests of the child. In this case, the application for authorization shall include a written presentation of the educational project, a commitment to provide this instruction primarily in French, as well as documents proving the ability to provide family instruction."

These few changes to the Education Code are intended to set out guidelines for and better control home schooling. It is granted for a period of one year, renewable in case of health problem or disability of the child. The reinforcement of the conditions and controls aims to avoid the de-schooling for false personal reasons or linked to cultural and religious separatism. Henceforth, home schooling cannot be carried out without the authorization of the competent State authority, which will watch out for anti-republican drifts and abuses.

---

7. https://www.legifrance.gouv.fr/jorf/article_jo/JORFARTI000043964862

School accommodations

The CNED

Home schooling should remain a last resort in cases of anxious school refusal. It is reserved for manifestations of anxiety and severe phobia that cannot be alleviated by treatment and school arrangements. If none of this allows a progressive return to school, if the clinical condition does not improve, it is necessary to consider this radical measure which can only be temporary. Another determining factor in the decision to follow a CNED curriculum is the child's ability to adapt to this form of solitary teaching which requires autonomy, discipline in the rhythm of work, perseverance and a certain clinical comfort, i.e. with a reduction in anxiety and depression, often associated, which does not alter cognitive abilities too much. It is a decision that is made after careful consideration with the child and parents, and after evaluation of the aptitudes for this demanding course. The other condition is not to isolate oneself at home, and certainly not alone in one's room except to work. If the phobic anxiety is centered on the school, it is always possible to envisage outside activities, and if possible with other children. If it is dangerous to drop out of school, it is even more dangerous to become unsocial. Moreover, a sedentary lifestyle is contrary to clinical well-being, which requires physical and creative activities in a context of relative sharing with people.

The CNED was created during the Second World War in order to establish a distance learning service. What was only meant to be a temporary solution proved to be useful in many situations where it was impossible to be present in a school. It is quite naturally that it has found its place in the educational landscape, in agreement with the Minister of National Education to ensure the quality of learning. Thanks to the evolution of digital technologies, and even more so to the Covid pandemic, the growth of the CNED has made it an efficient service that has become indispensable. Some students and parents appreciate distance learning as long as it is of high quality. However, during the pandemic, the distance learning offer was very disparate, depending on the teachers and the schools. Some students were well monitored with homework, sometimes even more, sometimes too much. Others were lost, with no work to do, in the chaos linked to technological malfunctions and the inability of teachers to adapt to this new situation that disrupted their teaching. One cannot blame them, as they themselves were under pressure to adapt personally and professionally without sufficient availability or means, unlike the CNED.

The CNED method, when deliberately chosen, is based on three axes.

"Wherever I want: I can work at home, at my workstation, etc. I am no longer obliged to travel or to take accommodation near my training location. When I want: I organize my schedule according to my personal and professional activities. I am no longer dependent on fixed schedules that are difficult to reconcile with my constraints. As I wish: I study at my own pace according to my level and my objectives. I am free to work more specifically on a sequence or to quickly go over concepts already acquired.

This freedom, between personalization and individualism, does not always correspond to an education provided to the student who is suffering and will have to return to an institution as soon as possible. The student's freedom is not to *do where I want, when I want and how I want.* He is offered a quality service but out of spite because no other solution has been found. This apparent freedom comes at a price both for the parents who must make themselves available and for the child who works in solitude. Not sure that this status is enviable... nothing to do with the freedom to come and go when one is well, and the austere, even autistic, one who had no other choice but to flee the school.

There are a number of reasons why a child may not be able to attend school, including hospitalization or intensive medical care, a pathological situation or a disability recognized by the Commission des droits

et de l'autonomie des personnes handicapées (CDAPH), which is part
of the MDPH. As we have seen, it may also be due to the need for high-
level sports or artistic activities that do not allow the child to follow a
traditional curriculum, but one must be extremely careful about this
type of choice for a child whose priority must be to discover life and
learning with and among others. In these situations and in general, it is
preferable to think of an adjusted education with a partial schooling in
an institution, associated with a CNED curriculum. Unfortunately, this
is not always possible, especially when the child moves around a lot,
and, for our purposes, if the anxiety is too great.

There remains the worrying situation of students with disabilities
or psychiatric pathologies who cannot benefit from a satisfactory
inclusion despite the promise made to parents. They are faced with a
school management that is overwhelmed and without means, unable
to ensure the schooling of a child in great difficulty and who poses
behavioral problems. At best, the pupil is enrolled for a few hours
depending on the presence of AESH, people who are difficult to find
and train, often shared, which for children with great difficulties is
unthinkable. In these situations, the schooling is not the fault of the
parents but of the National Education. Should it be blamed for this? If
so, it is only making a promise that is impossible to keep: the inclusion
of all children, whatever their problem, in a traditional school environment. This is counterproductive for the child who is being schooled in a
dotted line, often stigmatized and suffering. It is counterproductive for
the education provided to other children.

There are other ways of thinking about social inclusion, in particular
by creating spaces and structures so that encounters between all
children are possible and profitable: play and theater spaces, creative and artistic activities, and many others to be invented by giving
ourselves the means, certainly costly but very profitable, to achieve it
(financial cost, specialized, well-paid and motivated workers, specific
training in inclusion without stigmatization...).

Find all the useful information

APADHE

Educational support at home, in the hospital or at school is a welcome initiative that requires a major commitment on the part of schools and teachers who are already very busy with lessons, preparations, tutoring, student evaluations and statistical assessments required by the French Education Ministry. These various and multiple tasks are in addition to their primary mission: that of teaching. In reality, this additional pressure and drudgery is the limit of this attractive offer for children who are ill or in great difficulty. It is however one of the links of the inclusive school which must adapt to particular situations and allow equity in the offer, if not equal opportunities. This involves political and social issues, and we have seen that the structure and programs of the national education system are far from achieving this equality. Nevertheless, the goal of inclusive schooling is to achieve true equity in provision, regardless of the psychosocial circumstances to which the child is subjected.

The partial or total inability to follow a school curriculum in an institution encourages and obliges the setting up of a program that will allow the student to follow the curriculum, but with personalized support from teachers and a close relationship, which is not the case with the CNED, which is only able to offer a distance learning program. The physical, psychological and social health of the child is at the heart of the Apadhe program, which offers academic and relational support that can be adjusted to the student's situation and needs. It requires the implementation of an individualized reception project, PAI. Each department is obliged to propose it, and its validation depends on the inspector of the academy and academic director of national education services (Ia-Dasen).

If everything goes smoothly, there will be no disruption in the child's schooling and in his or her relationships with teachers and students. On the horizon is the return to school that everyone hopes for, which will be all the better for the support provided during and after the return to school. All that remains to be done is to find a referent teacher who, even if designated by the Dasen, must be able to carry out this additional task in close coordination with the parents or the representative/legal guardian for a student in the child welfare system. Coordination is complex because it must take into account all the factors involved, the state of health and medical constraints, the pupil's academic level and difficulties, follow-up at home or in hospital, transmission, arrangements and contacts to be made according to the conditions. Ideally, one of the student's teachers should be responsible for this coordination task, provided that he or she agrees and is able to take on this function, which is certainly paid but goes beyond his or her duty time. It can also be a volunteer teacher specially dedicated to the transmission of lessons and school life, to the links with the students, to the evaluations and to the assessment with the child and his/her parents. This requires effective digital technology and practice, which avoid adding obstacles to the pedagogical difficulties.

If it is well conducted, we can see how this device can become the best in the situations of anxious school refusal mentioned in the chapters. An ideal system? Yes, but only if there is real coordination and commitment on all sides: the child, his/her parents or legal guardians, the coordinating teacher and the other teachers of the pupil, the quality of the digital offer, the empathy and availability of the school management, the teachers and the other pupils. In any case, it will always be better than a CNED course in the solitude and silence of one's room or a hospital room. This also presupposes, as is the case whenever special provisions are taken into account, the provision of additional resources and a real willingness on the part of the National Education System to ensure intelligent inclusion within or outside the curriculum in the school. Parents, legal guardians and the child's doctors must be aware of the modalities and demand the implementation of an Apadhe, as it is an integral part of the National Education's inclusion program.

Other facilities

2nd chance schools (E2C)

The E2C network extends throughout France and is experiencing significant growth. It has welcomed more than fifteen thousand young people without qualifications and without employment in 2021 by offering them an opportunity for socio-professional integration. The individualized training is aimed at young people without a diploma and those whose diploma does not allow them to obtain a job. This support is part of a youth commitment contract (CEJ), which is a step, a gateway to the professional future. Registration in an E2C is free. The young person has the status of trainee in vocational training and benefits in 2022 of a remuneration of about 500 € per month, financed by the Region according to his situation. The duration of the internship and the pedagogy used are variable according to the needs and the project of the young person which takes shape as the support is provided. This support ranges from motivation *coaching* to the choice of internships, and even to the job search. Training workshops, work experience, cultural and civic awareness, this offer is directly linked to the world of work and society. Thus, it avoids useless training with no outlet. To enter an E2C, in addition to the process with the local mission and the right to CEJ, it is possible to fill out an online application form, which will be sent to the E2C closest to the young person's home.

The micro-high schools

Another formula, the microlycee, allows a gradual return to school from the age of 16 to 25 for young people who have interrupted their schooling for at least six months. This light structure with a small number of students and adjusted attendance time is particularly well suited to situations of heavy absenteeism and dropping out before obtaining a diploma, particularly the baccalaureate. This alternative is ideal when a young person wants to return to school, even if he or she does not feel capable of doing so. There is always an individualized formula that will suit them. At the end of this training, he or she is able to take a baccalaureate in the same way as the integrated students, and not at a discount. The modalities of the micro-high schools, their courses of study and their pedagogical orientations vary from one school to another. However, the invariable features are the quality of the welcome, individualized teaching, empathy and benevolence. The number of students is reduced in order to allow for this alternative pedagogy. The emphasis is on participation in the group without forcing, knowing that a certain number of these students will be ready to flee at the slightest obstacle or criticism, due to anxiety, opposition or feelings of failure. The objective is to put the young person back at the center of his or her path and to reawaken his or her academic and professional motivations.

Without a relationship of trust, this committed and costly process may not succeed. Each student therefore has a mentor who is attentive to his or her obstacles, but also to his or her impulses, which must be seized before the feeling of failure, nullity or even distress arises. We must keep in mind that this distress can be disguised as opposition, escape or provocation. Teaching should not be boring, even if it follows the curriculum to get a degree. Intelligent pedagogies, such as that of Célestin Freinet, have proven that we learn much better when there is pleasure, sharing, active participation in a project. Without mentioning these methods that have proven their worth but that the French education system is reluctant to validate and develop, we can be pleased with this micro-school solution that saves a good number of young people who have dropped out of school, who have failed, who are depressed, and who feel so worthless. It is possible to join a micro high school if the student has been out of school for more than six months and has no prospects, but shows some motivation.

Innovative institutions

Grouped together in a federation (FESPI), the innovative public schools are few in number, about fifteen, and offer alternative pedagogies. They are the result of the thinking and experience of inventive educators who, in general, have worked in the field. They are experimental and are intended to enrich the pedagogy of traditional education. This requires considerable resources, but the results are encouraging. Teamwork, reflection on the project beforehand, assessment afterwards, participation of the students in the project and in decisions that concern them directly, close partnership with parents, motivated and curious teachers in a close-knit team. In short, this is all that is needed to successfully lead young people, with or without difficulties, towards the adult world. These establishments are evaluated and scrutinized in order to validate or not the pedagogies they propose. If the good recipes of innovative schools work every time, because they are based on active participation, pleasure and curiosity, one can ask why not develop them on a national scale. If their operation is more expensive than that of a classic establishment, this remains to be seen, because, all things considered, in the medium and long term, it is much more profitable for society if a young woman or man comes out of it able to take charge of his or her life, to find a job and to participate intelligently in civic life.

The relationship of trust between students and teachers, evaluations that do not take the form of judgments, the questioning of their methods by the students and the questioning of the teachers: all this does not prevent the exercise of authority and discipline in the pedagogical follow-up. The only regret is that these experiences are not more numerous in order to better respond to the problem of inclusion which concerns many students in difficulty, suffering, different, with high potential, or suffering from psychiatric pathologies which are not incompatible with an adapted schooling. Unfortunately, we see the opposite: some innovative establishments that are working very well are being moved or closed without any consultation with the teachers, staff, students and parents who are very much involved in these projects. This is enough to discourage initiatives and create bitter teachers.

The question remains as to what happens to these experiences. Do they feed into pre-service and in-service teacher training and in what way? What freedom do teachers have to apply these methods in traditional schools? Are they just a façade to silence the reproach of not being open to new pedagogies and to keep their defenders busy? The federation of these innovative schools is working to ensure that traditional schools benefit from these experiences and become places of pedagogical and human innovation. The testimonies of teachers, parents and students from traditional schools say that they do not really see the color of these innovations, except in the micro-schools, which only concern a few students who have already dropped out of the system.

It is regrettable that there are only fifteen innovative institutions. This means that places are expensive, especially since education is free, a paradox. If there is one of these establishments close to the home of a child in difficulty, different, dropping out or even without any particular problem, it is an opportunity to be seized.

Non-contractual institutions

Private schools under contract are establishments that have signed a contract with the State and the National Education because they respect the clauses of approval. This allows them to benefit from government subsidies that support their operations. Therefore, even if there are tuition fees inherent to the private structure, these remain accessible to the middle classes. It is also possible to benefit from financial aid allowing access to the greatest number of students, even if the entrance fee remains a deterrent for some.

On the other hand, the non-contractual establishment is a school which has not signed a contract with the State, by choice, or more often by prevention on the initiative and prudence of the National Education, which cannot validate just any project and the drifts which can result from it in terms of content, pedagogy, risks of religious indoctrination or sectarian perversion. These establishments, if they are motivated by a desire to make progress in the pedagogy and personalized welcome of children, most often hope for a signature of approval which will be a guarantee of recognition and will limit the financial elitism of their access. Indeed, it is well understood that this kind of non-subsidized education is costly if its designers, as is often the case, do everything to ensure that a quality pedagogy is delivered while respecting the common base of knowledge, and this for a small number of students. I am not talking here, of course, about non-contracted establishments of sectarian or religious obedience whose aim is to reject secular republican education, judged to have gone astray, for the benefit of indoctrinating children.

Why offer a child a non-contract school? Some parents choose such a school from the outset, out of conviction, out of a choice to provide their child with a different pedagogical approach, out of a refusal of a teaching and education system that they did not experience well in their childhood, or because of word of mouth that praises the reputation of a school. More often than not, it is a second choice or a necessity for a child who is having difficulties, suffering, or who has behavioral problems adapting to the constraints of traditional schools and the normative rigidity of their pedagogy and teaching. And this often requires financial sacrifices to ensure the child's well-being, which the parents put first. In the situations described, we have seen the pitfalls of inclusion, which often lead to stigmatization and expulsive violence that traumatizes the child. One of the solutions to anxious school refusal is the possibility of enrolling the child in a welcoming school that accepts the difference, adapts its pedagogy and seeks to understand the student. This approach is beneficial because it helps to repair a loss of self-esteem, restores the confidence of the pupil and his parents, and therefore helps to unblock the situation of school withdrawal, a very damaging impasse for the child in terms of his psychological future and his social success.

Being a non-contractual school and wanting to remain so allows one to choose one's pedagogy without letting oneself be impressed by the controls of the prefect and the rector of the academy of the National Education who make sure above all that the director of the school and the teachers have the necessary diplomas. They also ensure that the school's operations respect public order, health and social prevention, and the protection of children and young people. They verify on the pedagogical level that the common base of knowledge and skills is respected, which is important in order not to harm the child in his or her school and university progress. However, the non-contract school chooses its teaching method, its rhythm, its programs in order to adapt them as well as possible to the student's progress. Therefore, as long as you check that the non-contractual school is not reported, it is possible to enroll a child directly in it, knowing that his or her schooling will one day lead him or her back to a traditional school because, very often, these establishments do not ensure continuity until the baccalaureate and university courses.

School support associations

The many tutoring services offered differ in their financial or volunteer orientation. On the one hand, there are organizations that provide tutoring in exchange for payment, in a variety of ways, on an ad hoc or regular basis. On the other hand, non-profit associations, whose workers are volunteers, focus on helping children in difficulty of all kinds (foreigners and migrants, students with difficulties from disadvantaged backgrounds and, more generally, families who cannot afford the assistance).

Difficulties in certain subjects, slight learning disabilities, dropping out of school, impossibility for families to ensure school follow-up, the contribution of these private or small group lessons is precious and favors equal opportunities by filling the gaps and restoring confidence to the student. These associations can be found in social centers and community centers, but also in charities and non-governmental organizations (NGOs). They receive subsidies from the CAF (Caisse d'allocations familiales) and from local authorities, provided they have signed a local contract to support schooling (CLAS).

Find all the useful information

Tutoring is most effective if the student is in the presence of the tutor, usually a retired teacher or volunteer with skills, but assistance can also be provided through digital technologies (online courses, video tutoring), which has proven successful during the Covid pandemic or geographic distance. Sometimes coaches travel to children's homes. It is important that volunteers be evaluated and that they have sufficient and appropriate training. Indeed, one does not improvise as a caregiver. Parents have had bitter experience of this when they themselves, having partly forgotten their school curriculum which, moreover, has changed a lot, want to help their child with his or her homework, or when they have recourse to a retired volunteer who has not updated his or her knowledge or teaching skills.

These numerous devices aim to adapt to the child when he or she fails to fit into a standardized school system that is intolerant of deviations from its norms. We need to find the one that best suits a child who is slipping, dropping out, suffering, or exhibiting anxious school refusal that drags on. There is nothing worse than letting a child drown, alone in the face of learning that is beyond him, without him daring to say so because he is ashamed of not being able to do it. They think it's their fault and that they suck.

However, it is established and confirmed by a good number of teachers, children and parents that the teaching and transmission of knowledge of the current pedagogy are very often out of touch. The complexification and abstraction of grammar rules, for example - but this also applies to mathematics, history, geography and physics programs... - leads to perplexity for both students and parents, who are confused by concepts that are as abstruse as they are ridiculously valuable. How to make complicated what can be simple, that's what the new program standards designed by the eminent certified pedagogues of the French National Education system come down to. Some teachers testify: "Why make simple when you can make complicated? In this respect, the prize undoubtedly goes to French, whose exhaustive and repetitive programs take a perverse pleasure in confusing the minds of students, their parents... and sometimes their teachers. The irruption into the programs (and therefore into the textbooks) of a jargon previously reserved for high-level students has been wreaking havoc since 1996. Not only have frighteningly technical terms flourished, but textbooks sometimes use more than one term to describe the same thing[8] . It is understandable that some parents make the choice, without their child having a problem, a difficulty, a difference, of family instruction. They choose for themselves what kind of teaching to offer, drawing inspiration from different pedagogical methods: Montessori, Freinet, Steiner. They want the best for their child without wanting to isolate him or make him into a prince, and they refuse to let him go through the mill of an elitist pedagogy, to be conformed and to lose the pleasure of learning. They refuse to subject him to the risk of betting everything on the school which, by its constraints, tends to devour the time and the pleasure of life. As we have seen, some parents have very questionable motivations for IEF, such as wanting to keep their child to themselves or not exposing him or her to an education they consider amoral. But other parents make an educational and life choice that aims at harmony and avoids elitist obsession, which does not prevent the child from succeeding. The child will even gain in psycho-affective fulfillment.

But IEF and CNED for a child in difficulty, with a tendency to become isolated, must be a transitional solution of last resort, with a more or less long term objective of a return to the school environment, whether it is traditional, alternative, out of contract, whatever, as long as it ensures a personalized and quality education.

---

8. DAVIDENKOFF E., and professors Bruno DESCROIX, Béatrice SALVIAT, Marie-Pierre DEGOIS, Emmanuelle THAUVIN-ROY, Karen GALLOIS, Alain BARBÉ, *Réveille-toi, Jules Ferry, ils sont devenus fous*, Oh!

How to meet a shrink

If shrinks are not the solution to all problems, they can be of precious help, provided that certain precautions are taken. The first concerns the practices and theories that support them. In other words, who does what and how? Before claiming to be a "shrink", what are the practitioner's training and diplomas? These are not an infallible guarantee of quality, but they are evidence of a duly validated training course. The interpersonal meeting that takes place with the parents and the child is, in a second phase, a crucial element of care. Trust is built through information on the practice and the progress of the care project, completed by the explicit agreement of the parents and the child. Patient rights apply to any professional who claims to take charge of, help or care for a child in difficulty and his or her family. If a strict code of ethics applies to doctors, other practitioners must demonstrate irreproachable ethics, especially since they are dealing with a child, who is by definition vulnerable and susceptible to influence.

Psychiatrists and child psychiatrists are doctors trained in the diagnosis and treatment of psychiatric pathologies, psychological suffering and trauma. Their supervised acts are paid for, advanced or reimbursed by social security. They are obliged to train throughout their career and must refer to their professional association. This is necessary as much for the evolution of treatments as for the psychotherapies they propose to their patients. Child psychiatrists are few in number, overwhelmed with work and caught up in the legal constraints of the High Authority for Health and government measures not always adapted to the reality of care. They are the only shrinks authorized to prescribe so-called psychotropic drugs that can be useful in the face of children's difficulties and pathologies. It is important that parents know who they are talking to. Indeed, some practitioners have a practice based on exclusive biological and genetic theories. They refuse psychotherapy and prefer to prescribe medication which, although useful as an adjunct to treatment, is not without risk for the child's development and metabolism. Other practitioners swear by psychoanalysis, refusing to take into account certain scientific data at the origin of learning or behavioural disorders, or which contribute to them. This split among psychiatrists is inherent in their history. It is detrimental to both the profession and to the understanding of disorders and their multifactorial and often interrelated issues. The choice of practitioner is an inalienable right in France. Therefore, depending on the meeting and what is proposed, parents are free to refuse and to refer to another practitioner, if only to obtain a second opinion. Child psychiatrists can be found in private practice, in medical-psychological centers (CMP), medical-psychological-pedagogical centers (CMPP), and in hospital structures (consultation and hospitalization, teenager's house...).

Psychologists follow a university training on two divergent axes according to their choice: psychopathology and neuropsychology. Here again, choosing one or the other is not trivial. Like doctors, they are bound by a code of ethics, to which must be added the respect of an ethic in the choice of their practice. Meeting with a clinical psychologist allows for psychotherapeutic help and care because the psychologist does not have medical training and is not authorized to prescribe medication. This does not prevent them from having received training in all neuropsychological pathologies during their studies. The concern for the families is that the sessions with the psychologist are not covered, with some exceptions: certain mutual insurance companies and, recently, a personalized plan within the framework of a disability procedure and the new "MonPsy" formula for the care of adolescents in difficulty, framed by a medical prescription, an evaluation and a limited number of sessions. The majority of psychologists refuse it because this very restrictive framework does not seem adapted to them. As for neuropsychologists, they are more and more numerous. This is linked to a desire to open up to neuroscience. But evil being the enemy of good, they are becoming unavoidable at the expense of clinical psychologists who favour a holistic approach taking into account all the data at the origin of a disorder (psychosocial, psychoaffective, but also neuropsychological).

The choice of neuropsychologists is privileged, even exclusive, due to the authoritarian and abusive orientation of the Ministries of Health and Disability, the High Authority of Health and the National Education on the TND, the neurodevelopmental disorder. Despite the absence of validated scientific data, the hegemony of this NDD covers all the alleged causes of learning and behavioral problems in children with difficulties. This leads to the multiplication of tests and assessments with the aim of confirming what is sought and will be considered a handicap. If the pressure is strong, a certain number of parents rightly resist, refusing that their children be subjected to various re-educations and drug treatments.[9]

Psychiatrists and psychologists are, because of their training, able to justify a title and practice of psychotherapist. They have the legitimacy to apply to the regional health agency (ARS), which has been required since 2010 in order to avoid abuse. The regulations allow one to find one's way through the constellation of psychotherapists and the diversity of their orientations, from psychoanalysis to meditation, from relaxation to EMDR, always on the condition that the training has been followed and validated, and therefore traceable for the patient.

---

9. DELCOURT Th., *La Fabrique des enfants anormaux*, Max Milo, 2021.

Psycho-practitioners, neither psychiatrists nor psychologists, come from various backgrounds, with rather eclectic orientations, from kinesiology to *gestalt therapy*, from *mindfulness* to hypnosis. They can be good therapists but it is very difficult to find their way around. Their studies are not subject to control but to validation by their training organizations. They are swimming in a nebula where the worst is next to the best. Caution is therefore required, which is a disservice to serious psycho-practitioners. It is essential to find out about their training, a possible sectarian report, with serious word of mouth and without proselytizing. They are not covered by social security or mutual insurance companies. The help - because we are not talking about care - is financed by the parents. So beware of miraculous promises, even if the magic efficiency still works in our society with scientific pretensions.

The offer of support by a psychologist is therefore wide and very diverse. If I may say so, there is something for everyone, or rather for every situation. However, this is reduced if we look at the ethical qualities of the practitioner, at his respect for professional secrecy, for the integrity and dignity of the young patient, without exerting a hold on him and his parents.

Even if psychological help has become commonplace, there is still a fear of the shrink linked to what myths convey - *if you go to a shrink, you must be crazy... shrinks, with their funnel, are crazier than their patients* -, linked also to the historical reality of psychiatry. Indeed, psychiatrists have the right, and have sadly abused it, to commit patients. They submitted to the pressure of public order and families until the law established a framework which, if not perfect, protects the freedom of hospitalized patients.

Another mode of defence in the face of the perception of the origin of their malaise and the risk to their mental health leads patients, particularly adolescents, to flee from this confrontation with the psychologist, hence their frequent comments such as: *It's useless, it's useless; I have nothing to say; I don't know, I have nothing to do here.* I hear this kind of talk very often. One must know how to overcome reluctance, fear and resistance with determination and patience. The solidarity of parents who have understood that their child has, deep down, a need to express what is weighing on him or her, is a precious and indispensable factor for successful psychotherapy.

We have seen how the shrink, just like parents and teachers, can be manipulated by the child who wants to escape the school environment at all costs and avoid confronting what scares him, what bores him or what requires an effort: *I'll see a shrink, but only if I don't go back to school.* It is not unusual for the consultation to start with this misunderstanding. The child lays down his conditions and will only speak in his immediate interest, unless the shrink dislodges him from his attempt to instrumentalize those around him. Skill is needed to avoid antagonizing the young patient who will gradually understand that his real interest does not coincide with his immediate interest. Not condoning his avoidance and refusal to go to school does not prevent us from understanding him and helping him to find the right solution to get back on track.

Collaboration between teachers, school management, school doctors and psychologists, parents and psychologists is the only guarantee of success in reattaching the child according to the right formula, the one that is possible for the child at this stage of his suffering or his opposition. If everything goes well, the first formulation that has become so frequent, *I have a school phobia*, becomes, for example: *I am afraid that my parents will divorce*, or: *I have been hit and I am afraid.* This is the beginning of the unfolding of what led the child to flee the school environment. More and more often, I find that pre-adolescent children and teenagers ask for counselling or jump at the chance when parents suggest: *I've been waiting for this, but will it take away my fear?*[10]

It is obvious that, in these sometimes very serious sufferings, psychotherapy is an indispensable step, explicitly or implicitly requested by the child who is experiencing a situation that is often new and difficult

---

10. DELCOURT Th., *I am a teenager and I call my shrink,* Max Milo, 2016.

in his apprehension of the reality of the world. The different modalities of psychotherapy, in depth for an old situation, a trauma, an abandonment or any other upheaval of the child's unconscious, in support and as a mode of use, empowering him/her in front of a situation that he/she feels unable to face, or on the cognitive mode when phobic automatisms paralyze him/her... others still allow that a specific psychotherapy can correspond to each problem. One should not hesitate to leave a therapist whose psychotherapy is not adapted to the person's needs, or who has been stagnating for months without any tangible results. Otherwise, so much time is wasted!

There remains the prescription of medication, which is the subject of debate and fear on the part of parents, rightly or wrongly, between the fantasy of transformation of their child's personality and the reality of harmful effects when the prescription is not adequate, the medication not being adapted to the age of the child, to his or her situation, or being used in abusive dosage. This does not mean that all medications should be demonized. Strong anxiety, whatever the age, needs to be soothed. Taking a good anxiolytic is preferable to the trauma induced by anxiety. Similarly, if sleep disorders lead to exhaustion, the child is caught in a downward spiral that leads to depression. It is necessary to help him sleep, we use then an anxiolytic or melatonin. If a child is trapped in an impulsive state that endangers others and himself, it is sometimes necessary to use a drug that helps him control his violence by acting on the sudden emergence of his impulses. A mild dose of a neuroleptic is preferable to excluding and stigmatizing the child for his or her behavior. Similarly, a severe depressive pathology may emerge in childhood. It obliges to prescribe an antidepressant associated with an anxiolytic in order to relieve the child even if this cannot cure him. It is not for the sake of it that a psychotropic drug is prescribed to a child. It is always useful if another approach is not enough to soothe the child, but then one should not hesitate to do so because his malaise can become unbearable and lead him to suicide. Here again, there is no dogma but a pragmatic realism in order not to aggravate the disorders. If the prescription must be spread out over a short period of time, it is not advisable to stop a psychotropic drug abruptly at the risk of withdrawal symptoms or a relapse. Indeed, as much as there is a time lag between its prescription and its action, stopping a drug can be premature, with the equally delayed recrudescence of symptoms. This decision to stop the drug requires careful evaluation. In summary, there is no reason to prescribe a drug without accompanying it with intensive psychotherapy, which remains the central approach to the care of the child and adolescent, but when justified, this prescription is a very valuable aid.

BIBLIOGRAPHY

Calvino (Italo), *Le baron perché*, Paris, Seuil, 1960 (exists in coll. pocket).

Davidenkoff (Emmanuel), *Réveille-toi, Jules Ferry, ils sont devenus fous*, Oh! Éditions, 2006.

Delcourt (Thierry), *La Fabrique des enfants anormaux*, Paris, Max Milo, 2021.

Delcourt (Thierry), *Je suis ado et j'appelle mon psy*, Paris, Max Milo, 2016.

Delcourt (Thierry), *When the crisis becomes an opportunity*, Eyrolles, 2018.

Dubet (F.), Duru-Bellat (M.), *L'école peut-elle sauver la démocratie*, Seuil, 2020.

Eliacheff (Caroline), Masson (Céline), *La Fabrique de l'enfant-transgenre*, Éditions de l'Observatoire, 2022.

Fontanieu (Jérémie), *The School of Reconciliation*, Les liens qui libèrent, 2022.

Frochaux (Claude), *Aujourd'hui, je ne vais pas à l'école*, Lausanne, L'Âge d'Homme, 1982.

Huerre (Patrice), under the direction, *L'Absentéisme scolaire*, Paris, Hachette, 2006.

Huerre (Patrice), *Adolescentes - Les nouvelles rebelles*, Paris, Bayard, 2013.

Landman (Patrick), *Tous hyperactifs?*, Paris, Albin Michel, 2015.

Melman (Charles), Lebrun (Jean-Pierre), *La Dysphorie de genre*, Toulouse, Eres, 2022.

Meirieu (Philippe), *Apprendre... oui, mais comment*, ESF, 1992 (9th edition).

Meirieu (Philippe), *La Riposte*, Paris, Autrement, 2018.

Pellissier (Jérôme), *La Fabrique des surdoués*, Paris, Dunod, 2021.

Pennac (Daniel), *Chagrin d'école*, Paris, Gallimard, 2007.

Sciara (Louis), *Banlieues*, Eres, 2011.

Stora (Michaël), Ulpat (Anne), *Hyperconnexion,* Paris, Larousse, 2017.

Valet (Gilles-Marie), Lanchon (Anne), *Moi, j'aime pas l'école*, Paris, Albin Michel, 2005.

Viaud (Marie-Laure), *Une école différente pour mon enfant?*

Zerrouki (Rachid), *Les Décrochés*, Paris, Robert Laffont, 2022.

Zerrouki (Rachid), *Les Incasables,* Paris, Robert Laffont, 2020.

ABBREVIATIONS AND ACRONYMS

AESH: accompanying students with disabilities, presence with the student.

APADHE: educational support at home, in the hospital or at school.

AVS: school life assistant, help with the integration of the disabled, now AESH.

CNED: Centre national d'enseignement à distance (National Center for Distance Learning), an offshoot of the French National Education system.

DYS: dysfunction of multifactorial origin that can affect various functions, language, writing, calculation, sensorimotor, with consequences on learning.

ITEP: Therapeutic, educational and pedagogical institute, a medico-social establishment.

MDPH: Departmental house for the disabled, centralizes requests.

RASED: network of specialized assistance to students in difficulty, to counter school failure in kindergarten and primary school.

SAPAD: service d'assistance pédagogique à domicile, replaced by Apadhe.

SEGPA: adapted general and vocational education section, for students with significant academic difficulties, resistant to assistance and support measures.

SESSAD: special education and home care service.

TND: neurodevelopmental disorder, linked to early structural or functional lesions of the brain, with consequences of cognitive and sensorimotor alterations.

ODD: oppositional defiant disorder (DSM5) - irritable and angry child!

ASD: autism spectrum disorder, replaces PDD in the DSM5 classification.

ULIS: localized units for school inclusion, an inclusive schooling system for students with disabilities, combined with a period of traditional schooling.

ADHD: Attention Deficit Disorder with or without hyperactivity (DSM classification).

Table of Contents

Table of contents

Best sellers Max Milo Editions

Hitler's banker, Jean-François Bouchard

Confessions of a forger, Éric Piedoie Le Tiec

The Koran and the flesh, Ludovic-Mohamed Zahed

Governing by fake news, Jacques Baud

Governing by chaos, Collectif

A political history of food, Paul Ariès

Mad in U.S.A.: The ravages of the "American model",
Michel Desmurget

Mondial soccer club geopolitics, Kévin Veyssière

Putin: Game master?, Jacques Braud

Treatise on the three impostors: Moses, Jesus, Muhammad,
The Spirit of Spinoza

TV Lobotomy, Michel Desmurget

www.ingramcontent.com/pod-product-compliance
Lightning Source LLC
LaVergne TN
LVHW051157060726
842526LV00014B/3239